All of Us

Storytelling to Develop Critical Thinking in Sex and Relationship Education

Emmanuelle Cuccolo

"We Are A Rainbow. We Are United."
Cover Illustration by Jihad Chraa Ouarhrari

Dedication

For my mother and my daughter.

Acknowledgements

Firstly, I want to express my heartfelt gratitude to the wonderful women and LGBTQ+ individuals who have contributed to this project. Your shared experiences have not only enriched this work but have also taught me invaluable lessons in courage, kindness and hope.

Finally, I would like to thank my partner, Marc Dandridge, for his unwavering support. Thank you for your steady encouragement, your open-mindedness, and your genuine solidarity.

About the Author

Emmanuelle Cuccolo is an educator in gender, diversity and inclusion within higher education, specialising in gender equality and LGBTQ+ inclusion. She holds a Masters of Research in Sexuality and Gender Studies, and her research explores the impact of gender representations within Sex, Relationships and Health Education (RSHE) in England—specifically how these representations influence on gendered sexual behaviours and expectations among young people.

Emmanuelle is currently a PhD student in Health Services Management at the University of Birmingham, UK, deepening her research on gender representations within RSHE in England and investigating their impact on violence against women and girls.

"Storytelling reveals meaning
without committing the error of defining it."
Hannah Arendt

""Passion of experience" is a way of knowing that is often
expressed through the body, what it knows, what has been deeply
inscribed on it through experience."
bell hooks

"You can't deny that students have experiences
and you can't deny that these experiences are relevant
to the learning process."
Henry Giroux

Introduction

At the time I started thinking about this book, I was a 37-year-old woman. I had a 14-year-old daughter, Matilda, and I had started to think about the best ways to give her the right knowledge around sex. I wanted to support her and empower her to make the right decisions (I will return to this point in the section *My Learning as a Parent and a Human Being*, with some hindsight), not only during her adolescent years, but also throughout adulthood. Because, let's face it, adults haven't got everything worked out.

Soon enough, young people come to the realisation that their parents are most certainly not perfect, and that, as much as parents may try to give the impression that everything is under control and they have it all figured out, their children can certainly testify otherwise. In fact, even during the time I was working on this book, as a parent, I learned something important. Something huge. But before I tell you what that is, I must tell you a bit about me.

For decades, I was absolutely convinced that the cause of my troubled teenage experiences was the fact that I did not grow up with my mum. She died when I was four years old and my father is a good person, but he certainly was a difficult father. By the time I was fourteen years old I felt sad, angry and lost, but I was determined to take space in my life and to make the most out of being left to my own device. In part, that was an attempt to cover up the fact that I felt very lonely and uncared for. I did not feel like I belonged in my broken home, or anywhere else.

As an adult, I genuinely believed that all my bad choices in men were due to the fact that I had not received the guidance of my mother and her unconditional and eternal love. So, when I became a parent, I decided that I would absolutely be that mother for my daughter. I decided I would be the guiding presence that would protect my daughter from harm and from "undeserving and immature boys." I was so careful. I was so emotionally available. I felt belligerent about my responsibility – that was my mission. I was not going to let my daughter down. And yet, in time, things started to fall apart between us.

By the time she was two years old, I had had to walk away from the relationship with her father, and I immediately had felt the guilt of having given her "a bad start in life" in a broken family – like mine had been. And every single time she would get bullied or left behind by her peers in primary school, I would feel the inner mother-protector rising up in rage, ready to "put things right." Well, the paradox of wanting to be in control and not having any actual control over my daughter's life became apparent when she started secondary school and, aged thirteen, she decided to go and live with her every-other-weekend father and his new wife. And this was not a case where parents are able to co-parent wisely and in partnership for the greater good of the child – quite the opposite, unfortunately.

This was rather a case where her dad was trying to hurt me by manipulating his own daughter against me at a vulnerable age.

No one can imagine what that did to me. Up to that moment, I had blissfully been my daughter's mother; I had been on my mission, trying to protect her from pain and hurt, and enjoying our life together. And suddenly, I had a lot to figure out in terms of what was left of my identity as a person, and how I was going to parent her from a distance as the weekend-parent. I came to the realisation that my becoming a mother had only temporarily cured my love-hungry heart and filled the black hole in my chest. A hole that, contrary to what people may think, did not miss my mother less and did not become smaller in time, but bigger. When my daughter came into the world, the hole had filled with love and light, and the mother-daughter relationship was finally to be—only I was the mother, not the daughter. But, with Matilda leaving my home at the age of thirteen, I had to figure out how to be there for her, whilst desperately attempting to keep it together as my heart was breaking.

During this time, Matilda had started to go through some challenging times, trying to figure out her identity and to fit in at secondary school. There was a lot of social experimenting on her behalf, and this was hard for both of us, as she was so stressed and burnt out that she would be very difficult at home. I remember feeling so frustrated and powerless, and I would often worry and wonder if she was going to grow into a person with the necessary internal resources to keep herself safe and to make the right decisions for herself. All I wanted to know was that she would be alright in the end.

Through these very difficult years, something unexpected happened: because I was no longer the parent stuck in the role of ensuring she had cleaned her room, done her homework and returned home in the evening at the agreed time, new possibilities appeared on the horizon in my parenting role—I could be more of a mentoring parent for her. All along, I had been planting the seeds for my daughter to know she could always talk to me about anything, including sex, because I simply would not shy away and would be open to questions.

During that time, I would welcome, and even initiate, conversations about boys, girls, sex, contraception, masturbation, pornography, female empowerment, role models and fake role models. We would rarely agree on the latter, but the door was always open for those conversations.

During our many conversations, I was brought back to my teenage years, and I noticed that some aspects of my experience matched the narratives of her current experience, but some really didn't. I remember, as a teenager, forever worrying about the way I looked, the way I dressed, I spoke, I smoked—even the way I ate— as in, *"Would I look like a nerd if I suddenly sank my teeth into an* apple whilst hanging out with my friends?" or "Do my friends realise that my clothes are second-hand?"

Existing as a teenager was a full-time job, and an awkward one. Being stuck between childhood and adulthood, between games and responsibilities, between having the best laughter with friends, anytime, anywhere—and then wanting to die for finding out an embarrassing rumour about me had been spread. It was exhausting.

Most of all, I learned a lot about the current state of affairs amongst teenagers: anything from new sexual behaviours, to the influence of pornography on the culture of sexual relationships in secondary school, to the pressure to have a vulva that looks like the ones featured in sexist, misogynist pornography or mentioned on social media, to the temptation of looking at plastic surgery as some kind of workout plan and a tool in the project of becoming a woman.

These issues clearly did not exist back in my days—the nineties—because we did not have social media or the internet, and we could not access porn as and when. I can remember, as a teenager, often finding ripped pornographic magazines around isolated beaches, in the countryside, or even on city pavements, and I remember trying to piece the torn fragments of paper together to outline the naked bodies, hoping (and dreading at the same time) to see some nakedness: some bushy-looking genitals, or some natural, average-sized and average-shaped breasts.

Nowadays it's all completely different for teenagers—and, quite frankly, for many grown-ups too.

Suddenly, I felt my daughter was standing on a beautiful beach before an aggressively advancing tsunami of pressure from everywhere: pop music videos, porn and social media alike were inundated with pressure to be sexy, perfect, and ready to have all the wildest sex at all times.

Really, what's that all about?

It seems young people are now constantly judged according to their body being more or less similar to the current configuration of feminine or masculine embodiment within very strict and oppressive body size norms dictated by current ideas of beauty in pop culture, the beauty industry, and the pornographic industry.

And I find this is particularly true for heterosexual young people.

In my time, you had to be skinny with a small bum but big boobs. Nowadays, you have to have a big bum, big boobs, but with a tiny waist—you have to have a super hyperbolic "hourglass figure," and if you don't have one naturally, you can just have plastic surgery.

In the jungle of filtered, pouting selfies, many young people try to create the illusion of being constantly sexed-up—regardless of how old they are, how they really feel about sex, or whether they have had any sexual experience in the first place.

Sure, the more one matures into adulthood and becomes self-aware, the less they are likely to care about what other people think of them. But it takes time. And when you are a teenager—well, time takes a long time.

How did I manage as a teenager?

All my best friends had the attention of boys or had a boyfriend, and I felt like I was always behind, trying to catch up on developing, both physically and socially. Until the game started for me too. Then, there was no stopping me from taking space in my life.

And I certainly had fun, but I also had some horrible experiences I wish I never had—because they didn't make me stronger; they damaged me. Yes, I do have some regrets.

Someone once told me: "Of course I have regrets! People who say they don't have regrets are either liars or stupid because that would mean that they have not learned anything from life!"

So, I guess regrets are part of growing up, and they teach us something about ourselves, about others, and about life in general.

And I genuinely did the best I could with no sexual and relationship education, and no support in a sexist and misogynist society. However, I believe there may be immense value in engaging young people in conversations where we can all say, "Me too!" or, "I also feel/felt that way!"—so that they, we, all of us, may feel less alone, and so that all of us may learn better ways to be there for each other in a way that feels authentic and real, and that empowers all of us to say:

"Together, let's change what hurts us."

Preface:
Self-Awareness, Empathy
And Gender Equality

As I started to study and research the topic of teenage sexual culture, girls' perspectives, boys' perspectives, womanhood, intersectional feminist theory and Queer theory, I noticed a peculiar reality: our sexual identity is intertwined with our sense of empowerment or powerlessness.

For instance, women have been largely subjected to the will of men in patriarchal systems for the last two thousand years. And the patriarchy is still operative today: in some countries, inequalities are imposed as part of a fanatical vision of society disguised as the true message of religious texts. In others, the patriarchy is entrenched in political systems disguised as republics or democracies, in which the state persecutes women through legislation that removes their bodily autonomy, denying or revoking their right to choose over their own bodies and their own life planning.

Ironically, in many of these countries, the pornographic industry isn't regulated, and people as young as children can access the most misogynistic and aggressive interpretations of heterosexuality, where women are portrayed as servile, disposable, rubber-made sexual objects that enjoy enduring physical abuse and aggression from men. In these states, rape culture is accepted, supported, and even protected, and yet the LGBTQ+ community—which is still fighting for the right to merely exist and love without boundaries—is prosecuted and discriminated against as an abomination against God.

There is an undeniable relationship between sex and power in the patriarchal world. Around the world, male polygamy persists. In some countries, women might pay with their life for so much as being accused of adultery. In some countries, female genital mutilation (FGM) is still practised to prevent women from feeling pleasure during sexual intercourse, with the excuse that this mutilation should guarantee women's virginity up to their marriage and prevent them from seeking sexual partners outside it.

The practice can result in infections, sterility, complications during labour, psychological, emotional, and physical trauma—and even death. The same practice does not apply to men. Moreover, throughout history, the rape of men, women, and even children has been a horrific weapon of war and slavery used by men to establish the power of one community over another. It seems that wherever there is an imbalance in social power, there is sexual inequality—to the point that sexual assault is used to establish dominance within a social hierarchy of injustice.

But we can observe another phenomenon throughout modern history: women all around the world have been standing up against the patriarchy and pushing back in different ways and for different reasons.

They have been marching for their right to vote, to own a bank account, to keep their surname after marriage, to study, to get equal pay, to choose over their own body, to access contraception and family planning resources, to end feminicide, to demand legislation to protect women from sexual violence and to prosecute sexual criminals, to end period poverty, to educate communities and challenge traditional practices of FGM, to protect their daughters, to proclaim the importance of adequate sexual education for all, to end sexual slavery, to stand against the sexual objectification of women, and to claim their right to walk the streets safely.

They have been reclaiming their rights, their identity, and their sexual agency as subjects rather than objects.

Alongside, the wonderful LGBTQ+ community has stood up for their rights—not only to be who they are, free from legal and social persecution, but to thrive with pride. There is an ever-growing number of wonderful people who are advocating for radical gender equality, celebrating Queer identities and promoting the empowerment of the LGBTQ+ community.

This community has an ever-growing number of allies, which means that more and more people have been literally unlearning the ways they were conditioned to feel about their body, their anatomy, their gender and sexuality—and have been learning and figuring out an alternative way of existing, feeling self-confident and empowered.

We have not yet achieved radical gender equality for all, and the journey is challenging. But participating in this movement is truly mesmerising—and life-changing—to experience.

Toxic Masculinity

Society has, in recent years, started to examine toxic masculinity. This term refers to certain traditional gender stereotypes and harmful cultural norms attributed to men, where they are expected to be socially dominant, physically overpowering, emotionally illiterate, forbidden to cry or show any form of fragility or vulnerability, naturally inclined to objectify women, and eager to sexually harass women whenever they can get away with it. It also includes promoting or turning a blind eye to violence, including sexual assault and domestic violence, along with possessing innate traits of misogyny and homophobia.

The unlearning of these cultural norms—through both education and challenging conversations—is crucial to the wellbeing of people of all genders, including cisgender, heterosexual men. It must be acknowledged that toxic masculinity is incredibly harmful to men as well. In fact, the promotion of self-reliance and emotional repression within toxic masculinity is correlated with an increase in psychological problems such as depression, stress, substance use disorders, vulnerability to becoming radicalised, and, in extreme cases, even commit suicide.

In summary, the lack of gender equality, the influence of pornographic sexist narratives, the commodification of people's insecurities on social media platforms, and the persistence of toxic masculinity are negatively impacting all genders.

Consequently, the opportunity to develop critical thinking, self-awareness, and empathy—and the practice of gender equality—is needed more than ever. Challenging prejudice, fostering self-discovery, and promoting self-love are skills that serve all people, regardless of their gender or sexual orientation.

This Anthology

What I have been asking myself is: why should people learn cultural, gendered behaviours from childhood, through adolescence and young adulthood, only to then be expected to unlearn them as they mature later in life? Why should adolescents be left to navigate the landscape of sexual experience without being equipped with the necessary knowledge and skills?

No young person is expected to just get into a car and start driving among other experienced or inexperienced drivers when they have not been taught how the car works and what the rules of the road are. So why are they expected to engage in sexual relations without being taught about their own body and the bodies of others? Would it not be better for them to be enabled to develop self-awareness and the ability to respect and empathise with others, so as to spare themselves—and others—from negative sexual experiences or sexual trauma?

Why isn't Sexual, Relationship and Health Education (RSHE) planned and delivered in ways that empower young people from the grassroots? Why aren't they offered the strategies needed to learn more about people's differences and similarities in ways that foster respect and safety? How can learning about their body, needs and desires be scaffolded in RSHE? How may they acquire the ability to attune to their own sexual personhood, whilst not diminishing the personhood of others?

In this anthology, I have collected real stories of sexual encounters that took place during the adolescence of real people. I have interviewed participants about both positive and negative sexual experiences, to offer real contexts and facilitate teenagers in identifying with the people in the stories. The aim is to deeply engage young people in recognising key issues and to ignite meaningful discussions with peers, educators and parents.

It is common knowledge that teenagers find talking to their parents about sex—or hearing them talk about sex—very icky. Parents are generally not that keen to know too many details about their children's sex lives either. Incidentally, this barrier often results in teenagers knowing very little about real sex, and a lot about unrealistic, aggressive and unsafe sexual practices featured in mainstream porn.

This avoidance attitude towards sex education is completely unnecessary and, frankly, obsolete. It has been the source of countless traumatic sexual experiences throughout history. It is also incredibly anachronistic in this day and age, when intersectional feminist and Queer social movements continue to face issues such as incest, rape culture, systemic sexual harassment, discrimination and exploitation, child-on-child sexual violence, and general ignorance around matters such as consent and safety.

I join the intersectional feminist and Queer movements in calling for a culture of transformation, urging adults and teenagers alike to engage in conversations on these important issues. I urge everyone to sensibly overcome any sense of embarrassment or shame, allowing for a more honest collaboration within safe contexts where all sides feel comfortable and willing to learn from one another.

Discussing other people's choices—when there can be no negative repercussions on them, as in the case of this anthology—can create fertile ground where educators and teenagers can safely try to place themselves in somebody else's shoes and reflect on their own practices and beliefs around sex. It also offers a chance to critically explore what motivates people to engage in sexual acts.

Having a chance to compare the stories in this anthology with anything young people might have experienced—or are currently experiencing—could prove to be an effective RSHE pedagogical tool. It could dramatically broaden the scope and content of conversations around sex. The hope is that the conversations sparked by these stories may have a direct and positive impact on the lived experiences of young people, improving their overall physical and mental health. In doing so, these conversations could also help to prevent violence against women and girls, reduce harassment of the LGBTQ+ community, and support the development of self-awareness and empathy in young men.

Recruiting Participants

When I started recruiting participants, I decided to approach various feminist groups on social media, but only one local feminist group granted me an audience during one of their monthly meetings. I was only able to pitch this research project to the meeting coordinators and not to all the present members. I explained that the intent was to engage adults and young people in conversations about teenage sexual experiences through anonymous storytelling, with the aim of providing contexts for young people to connect some of these stories to their current circumstances and reflect on issues of safety and meaningful connection. However, I felt very defeated by their reactions and responses, which can be summarised as suggesting that we all had to go through some kind of bad or traumatic sexual experience as teenagers, as though it was some rite of passage to sexual adulthood. I was astonished by this level of apathy and felt sick to my stomach. As the group coordinators tried to oversimplify the matter, implying that my attempt was of no consequence in the grand scheme of feminism, I could hear myself shouting in my head, "No, it doesn't have to be this way!"

I left them and their members, who were moulding clay balls containing flower seeds to be disseminated around the neighbourhood to facilitate the growth of wildflowers and nourish the bees, feeling sad. To my surprise, other local feminist groups did not even reply to me.

I also reached out to my friends on social media, but not to all of them. I selected those I felt might have an inclination for philanthropy, were parents like me, or were close friends from my youth. I was aware that, even if I was targeting potential interviewees according to these criteria, it would not be easy for people to open up to me and talk about something so private. But I am an optimist, and talking about sex has never phased me. On the contrary, I've always found this topic fundamentally natural.

In terms of friends responding to me on social media, a couple answered, "Absolutely not, thank you!" and the majority did not respond. Some friends were forever busy, promising to schedule the interview at some point in the future, and only a small number agreed to take part in this project.

Interestingly, my closest friends refused. I knew well some of the experiences they had as young women because, on many occasions, we had talked about them over and over. I found their contributions and viewpoints would have been so precious for the intent of this book, but when it came to making a decision, they told me it was too painful for them to recount those experiences or that it was not their "thing." I was surprised and a little lost for words. I did not want to cause my friends to suffer or become upset, but then I realised that, well into their thirties, forties or fifties, they were walking around carrying an enormous amount of pain and shame deep inside them. To me, that was even more revealing of the consequences of neglecting sex education in adolescence, setting them up to pay a high price for the shortcomings of the adults and educators who should have supported them. I felt sad that my friends missed the opportunity to participate in a project meant to emancipate and educate young people so that they could be less likely to suffer in the same way we had. I also felt deeply sorry for their inability to show compassion to their younger selves. I would leave feeling overwhelmed by a sense of real urgency as to why this project, and many more, are needed. Each time, I would go home more focused and determined to find a way to recruit other volunteers, somehow.

The people who volunteered to take part in this anthology all happen to be Queer or cisgender women, so one might wonder why I have not included men. I can't deny that I would have preferred to have cisgender men involved in the collection of stories as well, to gain their valuable perspectives, but no man reached out. The reason could be that most men might not recognise the need to change the status quo around sex and relationship education in this culture, or they may not have the self-confidence and courage to get directly involved in this topic. This only tells me that many men and young men need support and for their confusion and lack of certitude to not be neglected or misjudged.

However, one might argue that this anthology may only be relevant to cisgender and LGBTQ+ women, not young men, but I strongly disagree. I find that the points for reflection identified in each story encompass challenges and fragilities that pertain to all human beings. We are a lot more similar than we are different, and all of us should be supported and encouraged to access our full range of human emotions, free from gender stereotyping.

The friends, friends of friends, or members of social media feminist groups who accepted to participate in my project, as I sometimes took part in theirs, absolutely blew my mind. With each interview that took place, I witnessed the most intimate and poignant aspects of sexuality and sex being brought to the surface with grace, compassion and wisdom in a unique way by each person. These interviews took place over a process stretched out in time—years, in fact—but it somehow felt to me like a harmonious symphony, where each instrument played a vital role in the production of the final composition. Each melody and rhythm melted into a wonderful and vulnerable collage of human experience. I felt so honoured by the trust and confidence the participants gave me, and I was humbled by their generosity.

Working on this anthology, I asked my interviewees to talk about the best and worst sexual experiences they had as teenagers, paying particular attention to the social and cultural factors that contributed to making the experience one they remembered with fondness or one they remembered with sadness or anger—or any other feeling. I also asked them to share useful insights, the pearls of wisdom they would have liked to have received as teenagers but never did, and that they would like to share with other young people today.

To facilitate the process, to create a safe place, and to honour the confidence and openness offered to me, I also shared an experience of mine with them in each interview, which I have anonymously included in this book, thus taking part in the courageous and generous act of vulnerability that is real storytelling.

My Learning as Parent and a Human Being

Interestingly, one of the friends who did not agree to contribute asked me why I wanted to write this book. Being a psychotherapist, she asked, "Is it possible that this is a way to come to terms with what happened during your turbulent adolescence?" I had never thought about that possibility before. I did not know. I answered that I didn't think so.

Yet, with each time I heard these incredible people's stories and their precious pearls of wisdom, and with each time I repeated my experience to them in something that became a ritualised possibility for self-compassion—the good and the bad—I felt I was finally paying attention, lots of it, to my wounded, isolated teenage self, who had dealt with sexual trauma all alone—which meant not dealing with it at all.

She also asked me, "Is it possible that you are committed to this project to compensate for the fact that your daughter does not live with you anymore, and you need to fill the void and exorcise the anxiety you have about the fact that she might make unsafe decisions?" I felt a sting in my stomach. Of course, I had been discussing with my own psychotherapist my struggles as a parent and my feelings about motherhood. Psychotherapy has been extremely important and transformative for me. I have learned that, no matter how much you want to protect your child and offer them the teachings you had to learn the hard way, they are their own beings. They are bound to learn not through theory imparted from parents and educators, but through making mistakes and through experience (and this was the great learning curve for me, the one I've mentioned in the introduction).

However, one way to support her was through empowering her—through facilitating a habit to think critically about herself, others, and sexual gendered behaviours and expectations, and through supporting her in practising self-awareness and empathy towards others. Yes, this was also a way to be close to her and love her, no matter what, even from a distance, even if she would not listen to my advice. It was a way to make the entire world a better place, for her. And although it could take me years to publish this book, and by then Matilda would be all grown-up, this book could serve, even just a little, all the young, wonderful and promising Matildas out there, whatever their gender identity, sexual orientation, and even age.

During this difficult time, I started to have psychotherapy, and this proved to be the gamechanger: the beginning of my healing and my becoming the main character in my story at last. Through this work, that continues to this day, I was able to catch up on the development that I had not been allowed in my upbringing. It is has gradually become clear to me that it wasn't my daughter's life purpose, nor anyone's for that matter, to make sure I felt loved and whole. It was mine and mine only.

Disclaimer

I have not written this book claiming to have all the answers to the infinite questions about wonderful and safe teenage sex. We are all different individuals with varying sexual preferences, desires, and background stories. There are also people who do not experience sexual desire, and yet even asexual people are on a spectrum. But I do believe that, as human beings, we can forever grow to be more truthful to ourselves, and that we can learn to honour our values while respecting others. This truly is a life-long journey! I do not claim to know what is best for everyone.

We live in times of incredible social change, and I believe that young people have played a key role on many levels: from the unprecedented political campaigning to save the planet, calling out our politicians to act on climate change, to their incredible response to the #MeToo movement, to their readiness to participate in and lead the #BlackLivesMatter movement, to their soulful and untamed commitment to breaking the social restrictions on "acceptable" gender identities, binary norms, and heteronormativity. This young generation is proving to be deeply self-aware and has a magnificent vision for change. And this is exciting to witness, and deeply inspiring.

I was a teenager who found it very hard to navigate the landscape of sexuality and early sexual experiences. I have spoken to many people—friends, strangers, and family members—and I have spent years researching and studying sexuality and gender. Through this, I have come to the understanding that things around sex are likely to be very confusing when you are young. In addition to the physiological and developmental turmoil of adolescence, nowadays there is the ever-growing prominence of social media's distorted representation of sexuality, body image, gender roles, and female beauty standards as some kind of "currency." Not to mention the 24/7, age-unrestricted access to the cringing misrepresentation of sex in mainstream pornography.

It is time for adults to be willing to engage in a conversation where they can offer a safe place for young people to express themselves, to ask questions, and to trust that adults will not be judgmental but will be on their side. It is time for adults to express empathy and solidarity with teenagers and offer them honest, practical answers, prioritising their wellbeing and safety. The main objective of such conversations should be to enable young people to feel confident, to value who they are, to empower them, and to enable them to become conscientious, responsible, and to enjoy sex safely and respectfully. The aim of writing this book has not been to provide all the answers, but to provide a resource that can be used to facilitate constructive conversations where we can all learn from each other.

Guidance in Reading this Anthology

Facilitators of these conversations should open each session by asking participants not to recount any personal stories of sexual relationships or hook-ups, nor to disclose the identities of sexual partners, or discuss other people's experiences while identifying them to the group. They should be encouraged to discuss opinions, ideas, and points of view in a theoretical way and in relation to the stories featured in the anthology, rather than in relation to specific people known to the group.

It should be clarified in advance that if any participant needs advice because they are worried about someone they know, or if they need support themselves, they will be provided with a variety of options to seek support privately and safely from the facilitator. Participants should be supported to report any instances of rape or sexual assault to the appropriate professionals privately—if they decide to do so—as any graphic description of such crimes could trigger distress in other survivors of rape present in the room during the discussion.

All participants need to know they are welcome to leave the discussion at any time without having to explain why, and provisions must be made in case anyone finds any material upsetting or triggering in any way. It is also essential that participants are offered a range of support tailored to their individual needs, including specific LGBTQ+ support, online organisations, local support communities, sexual health centres, police contacts, counselling services, and more.

Chapter 1
Feeling Your Body Is Celebrated

Adele 35, Italy

What was the best sexual experience of your adolescence?

The most beautiful sexual experience I had in my adolescence was at the age of 18 with a guy from Rome. He was a year older than me and worked as a tennis instructor in a tourist village in Calabria, where I was working at the bar. I remember feeling butterflies in my stomach that night when, after work, we met for a beer. After a couple of drinks, we shared a kiss, and I felt like I could touch the sky with my fingers. I really liked him, and I couldn't believe it when we finally kissed under the stars. I think I had idealised him a little, as often happens when you're a teenager, but he was brilliant! He was very focused on my pleasure, and I really wasn't used to that. The way he kissed me, caressed me, and licked me – can I say that? It was everything I had always desired sex to be.

Before this, I had not fully given in to my desires because I was inhibited by taboos, my shyness, and inexperience. I had never dared to ask for anything before. I still remember his big smile and how he took me by the hand, sharing this splendid experience with me. He made me feel comfortable, cared for, and he was passionate and gentle. It was during this very experience that I became acutely aware of the most intimate part of me that had never been explored. I felt celebrated in both my body and my soul.

Summary

- Feeling safe
- Feeling both excited and happy during sex
- Feeling a deep connection with your sexual partner

Points for Reflection

1. What does it take for you to feel safe during any type of sexual activity?
2. Is it important to feel safe?
3. Can someone feel happy during sex? Why?
4. What does it mean to you to feel celebrated during sex?
5. How do you know you have a deep connection with a sexual partner?

What was the worst sexual experience of your adolescence?

Today, I have a good rapport with sex, but it wasn't always that way. Let's say my first time (and I'm referring to penetrative sex) happened rather late compared to my friends. However, the most beautiful time wasn't necessarily the first time. I believe that for sex to be truly enjoyable, it needs to be experienced a little first. I'm not just talking about the physical act itself, but about getting to know our bodies and our pleasure through different experiences over time.

There were things I thought I wouldn't like, perhaps because of prejudice or inexperience. However, once I lost my inhibition, I discovered I actually liked those things a lot. Of course, what didn't help was that my early sexual partners didn't seem too concerned about my pleasure. I don't remember anyone actually asking if I had had an orgasm, and most times, it was implied that if a girl didn't have one during penetration, it was probably because she was frigid. But that's not true, as the vast majority of women I know don't have vaginal orgasms but experience them through clitoral stimulation.

There was certainly a lot of ignorance, both on my part and theirs, about what foreplay is and why it's essential for building a woman's sexual pleasure. I often felt that the traditional narrative suggested if things weren't happening in sex, it was usually the girl's "fault." So, I never wanted to make myself vulnerable to criticism, and I never addressed the issue of not having an orgasm. I never faked an orgasm, either, because I wasn't comfortable with that, though some of my friends told me they did.

Summary

- Sex can improve with time and experience
- Sexual inhibition
- Mutual sexual pleasure as opposed to a single individual's pleasure
- Foreplay
- Different types of female orgasms
- The shame of being labelled a 'frigid'
- Traditional female-blaming for not reaching an orgasm
- Faking an orgasm

Points for Reflection

1. Can the first penetrative sexual experience be beautiful, or is it bound to be painful for a girl or confusing for either partner?
2. What can be helpful to avoid feeling confused during sex?
3. What is sexual inhibition? Is it the same for everyone?
4. Is sexual inhibition "right" or "wrong"?

5. Is it possible not to be bothered about a partner's sexual pleasure during any type of sexual activity? Is that okay?

6. Is foreplay fundamental to build women's sexual pleasure and increase their chance to climax?

7. Does it take longer for women to reach an orgasm? If so, should they feel embarrassed about it?

8. Can pleasure feel different to different female individuals?

9. Is placing the blame on female partners for not reaching an orgasm common nowadays compared to the past?

10. Why do you think some girls might feel they have to fake having an orgasm?

11. What does this behaviour reveal about sexual expectations?

12. Did you know the only function of the clitoris, which is an organ, is sexual pleasure?

13. Did you know that even the vaginal orgasm is reached through the clitoris being stimulated?

14. Are you familiar with the anatomy of the clitoris? If not, take a look at these images.

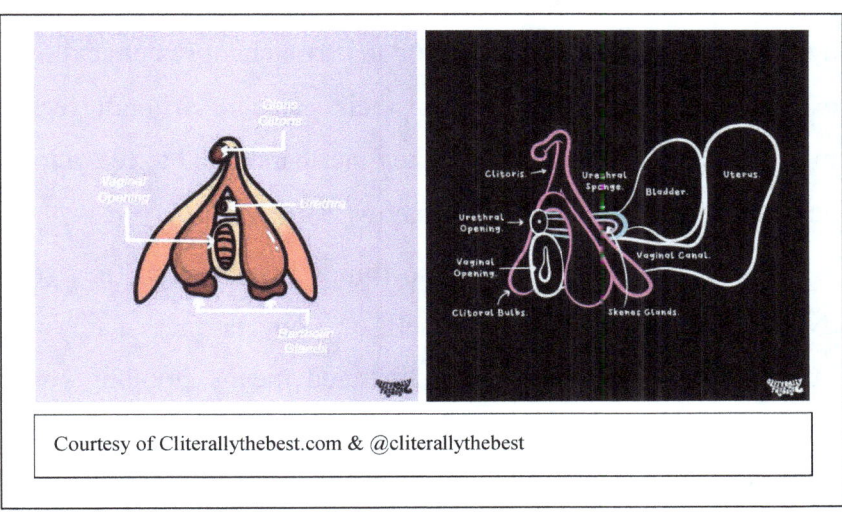

Courtesy of Cliterallythebest.com & @cliterallythebest

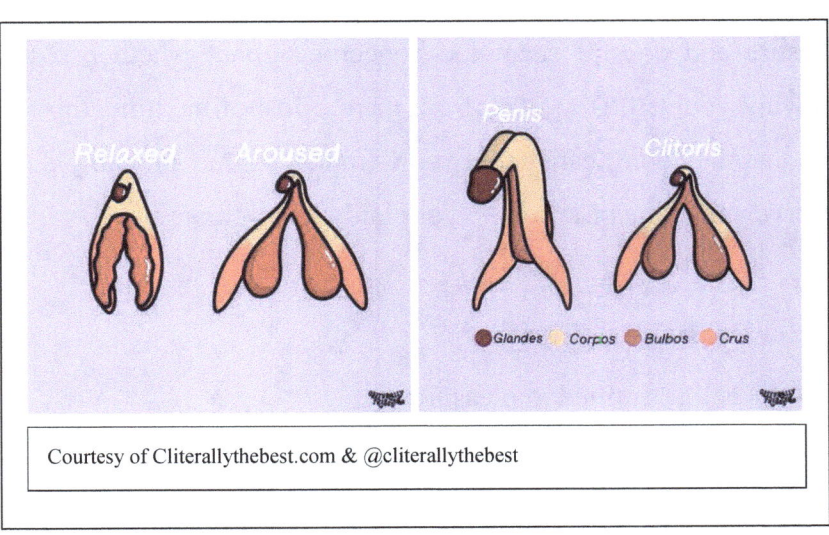

Courtesy of Cliterallythebest.com & @cliterallythebest

Adele's Insights

I would say, do not be afraid to ask. If you like something, suggest it to your partner. Boys tend to be much more demanding in sex, and generally, they go for their pleasure without feeling embarrassed or wrong. Girls, on the other hand, tend to feel a lot of shame and fear being judged somehow.

I'm not saying you should do things just because they seem adventurous, to prove to yourself or your partner that you're experienced or liberated. Being liberated means stopping caring about what others think of us, regardless of whether it's good or bad, and tuning in to ourselves. Go after what you like as well, and of course, make sure the other person consents first – it goes both ways!

I would also say that if a sexual partner is only focused on their pleasure and doesn't seem too concerned about whether you're enjoying yourself, stay away from them. Most of the time, this is a sign that they don't care about you as much, so they probably don't deserve your time or access to your body and intimacy.

Summary
- Feeling entitled to pleasure
- Being "free"
- Consent
- A selfish partner

Points for Reflection

1. Should anyone feel confident to communicate what they like to their partners?

2. Can having a deep emotional connection with your partner help to feel safe to open up about what you like in sex?

3. Are there any rules when it comes to being "adventurous"?

4. Is consent for boys too?

5. Can your partner be not bothered about your sexual pleasure but still care about you?

Your Notes and Critical Thoughts

_____

_____

_____

_____

_____

_____

_____

_____

_____

_____

_____

_____

_____

_____

_____

_____

_____

_____

_____

_____

_____

_____

Chapter 2
Sexual Harassment

Amélie, 31, France

What was the worst sexual experience of your adolescence?

Oh my God, what are you going to dig up?! Luckily, I did not have any terribly horrific experiences, but perhaps the one that hurt me the most was the one that happened with my step-brother at the time. I was 15, and he was 14. I was not in love with him or anything like that, but he stopped talking to me once he asked me to perform oral sex on him, and I refused. The fact that we obviously lived in the same house made it difficult for me because his negative behaviour was always there.

The second time he asked me, he actually followed me around the house, and he was so insistent that I ended up locking myself in the bathroom. When I refused to perform oral sex to him, he started to ignore me and pretend I was not in a room or that I was not talking to him, as if I did not exist. Or alternatively, he would bully me.

I had to realise that his interest in me was purely sexual and nothing else. I felt objectified as I was only ever going to be relevant to him to satisfy a sexual desire. There were no other feelings towards me. It was sad because when we were little, he had told me more than once that when we would be old enough, we would get married, so in a way, he had created a bit of a romantic context between us. But then, once we turned teenagers, he ended up exclusively pursuing a sexual act with me and nothing else. I didn't care about thinking of a romantic future with him. He had been the one to introduce some kind of expectations of some sort in me. But I did feel very confused about his change of attitude towards me, so even if I had not believed that we would end up getting married, he had repeated it enough times for me to at least think about it.

So, his selfish attitude towards me ended up making me feel very sad and have a very low self-esteem. I never said anything to my step-mum or my father, and I remember this was something I was always keen in hiding. I didn't want them to know because I didn't have any confidence that I could speak to them safely about any issue of this nature. Luckily for me, he started being interested in different girls at school and in the neighbourhood.

Summary

- Sexual harassment

- Feeling sexually objectified

- Being sexually harassed and feeling isolated

Points for Reflection

1. What is sexual harassment?

2. What do you think being sexually harassed feels like?

3. What does it mean to sexually objectify someone?

4. How can you make sure your partner does not feel sexually objectified?

5. Is sexual harassment and sexual objectification done to girls only?

6. What would you do if you were sexually harassed? Who could you talk to?

What was the best sexual experience of your adolescence?

I haven't had any positive sexual experiences in my adolescence.

Was it all been negative?

Honestly, it wasn't positive, and it wasn't negative. It was just an experience. This is because I've always perceived virginity as a stigma that I desperately wanted to get rid of because it made me feel inferior. My younger step-sister would call me "little virgin" as she used to get far more attention from boys, and she would be more interactive with them and have little dates. So, I experienced my virginity as a source of shame, like something that made me lacking somehow compared to others, like something that would place me at an inferior level. I felt inferior because I hadn't had that type of experience, as though 'someone' had decided that, at that age, you are supposed to have sexual experience. That was the norm, so because I did not conform to the norm, I felt I had something that wasn't okay, that I wasn't normal. And that is exactly how I felt about sexuality in my entire adolescence. So, any sexual encounter for me was merely an attempt to tick a box for society and to be seen in a certain way by others.

I had a relationship with a boy who was very much in love with me, so that ended up being a positive experience altogether, but not necessarily a positive sexual experience. Yes, we had ups and downs, and I surely knew he wasn't my soulmate or someone I would be with in the long term, but I knew for sure that he cared for me. Because he loved me, he made me feel important, and that is what I wanted in a relationship: I wanted to be important, and I wanted some attention because I didn't get any at home. So, on that level, the relationship was fulfilling.

However, I really thought I was a frigid woman because I didn't have any sensation during sex as I used to have sex just because I didn't want people to say those things about me, not because I felt mature enough to have it or because I wanted it.

I probably wasn't mature physically, and not even emotionally, because I had no idea what I really wanted. I ended up staying in that relationship because of the attention he was giving me. However, I believe I wasn't feeling any sexual sensation because I wasn't sexually or physically mature or into it.

I felt I was looking for someone I could never find, so I would have settled for anyone who treated me well and gave me some attention because if I didn't get any, it would mean that I wasn't normal and there was something wrong with me. So, in terms of sexual relationships or sexual pleasure, the only reason why I had sex in the first place would be to draw them close to me and get some affection. It was not because I'd find the experience pleasurable. It was a means to get closer to someone and look in them for something that I ultimately didn't have, like a father figure or any form of attention and affection I didn't get at home.

Summary
- The stigma attached to virginity
- Feeling obligated to "conform to the norm" and to tick the boxes

- Feeling no pleasure during sex

- Individual development

- Engaging in sex in order to feel loved and cared for

Points for Reflection

1. Is there still a stigma attached to virginity nowadays?

2. Is it worse for men or for women?

3. How is it for LGBTQ+ individuals or non-binary individuals? Is it different or the same?

4. Why do young people feel obligated to "conform with the norm" of being sexually active?

5. Who makes the "norms"?

6. Do people develop at different times psychologically, emotionally, physically and sexually? Is that OK?

7. Is engaging in sex a good idea when it does not procure any pleasure?

8. Is it possible that someone might not feel any pleasure because they might not feel safe? Or ready to have sex? What should they do?

9. Might there be a cost to engaging in sexual activity of any form just to "tick a box"? What might that cost be?

Points for Deeper Reflection

1. Are there historical reasons for virginity to ever become relevant?

2. Was it the same for everybody, men and women?

3. Do any of these reasons apply nowadays?

4. Does virginity mean the same to everybody?

5. How do you feel about the term "losing" your virginity, as opposed to perhaps "acquiring" something?

6. Does having sex to feel loved and to get affection work well or are there any risks?

7. Do you think young people from broken homes are necessarily more likely to have sex to feel less alone?

Arianna's insights

If I could go back, I would tell myself not to care about what other people say and that it is not true that if you haven't had sexual intercourse, you aren't an adult, you aren't mature, or you don't have life experience.

If you don't do it with the right person for the right reasons, the experience will end up not offering you anything valuable anyway. On the contrary, it will end up confusing you. Having X amount of sexual intercourse with X amount of people isn't important.

What's important is recognising your own feelings towards a particular person and understanding if you truly care about them or fancy them. It's better waiting to find a person that makes you feel that way, so don't settle for less, and don't get together with someone just for the sake of being with someone, for fear of being alone or for any other reason that doesn't really count, including being bullied. You are ready when you are ready. We're all totally different. We develop physically, mentally and emotionally at different times.

There are girls that get their period at the age of 12. I had my period at the age of 16, which was unusual compared to the rest of my peers. In my secondary school, most of my friends had already developed physically, had breasts and were tall, but I didn't, and I wasn't. Obviously, having a period doesn't mean you're sexually mature, but it's just an example of how people grow up at different levels and at different times.

Don't follow the herd. Don't be scared of being 'the black sheep'. And if someone bullies you because of who you are, they surely aren't your friend, so why would you care and be upset about what they think? Those people don't deserve your time and attention. And they might not even have all the experience they claim to have.

They act like that because they are bullies, not because there is something wrong with you. I didn't have anyone I could talk to about these issues, but if you do have a parent or, an uncle or, an auntie, or even a big sibling, talk to them and try to understand what is best for you.

Don't let bullies dictate how you should live and what you should do. When you have to decide what to do, try to tune in with who you are, how you feel and what you desire. And if you find it difficult, then take your time. Go deep in your thoughts, go deep in your feelings and understand what motivates you to do or not to do something.

I imagine that if I had had a mother figure who could listen to me and help me understand my own feelings, I would've recognised that I shouldn't have hurried to have sex just for the sake of it because I wouldn't have missed out on anything worthwhile.

Summary

- Motivations to have sex
- When in doubt

Points for Reflection

1. Is it important to understand your individual and genuine reasons for engaging in any type of sexual activity? Why?

2. Is it easy to understand what motivates us to have sex?

3. What sort of questions would you ask yourself to understand your motivations?

4. Is it important to understand your sexual partner's reasons for engaging in sexual activity with you? Why?

5. Is it possible for the mutual reasons to be not in alignment? Does it matter? Are there any problems or risks with that? Please try to explain.

6. Do you believe it may be good just waiting when in doubt?

Your Notes and Critical Thoughts

_____

_____

_____

_____

_____

_____

_____

_____

_____

_____

_____

_____

_____

_____

_____

_____

_____

_____

_____

_____

Chapter 3
Being Bullied and
Having Low Self-Esteem

Carol B, 42, England

What was the best sexual experience of your adolescence?

I had a really good time up to when I was twelve. I had loads of really nice friends and had a great time at school. Then I had the worst time until I was about 15, and then it got much better. But those years were so critical that they had a really big impact on my self-esteem. I had a really nice family and really nice friends outside of school, but I got bullied by a lot of people. It was all verbal, including people I didn't know who would call me names all the time in my school, and what it meant was that because I got on really well with my family, I felt really loved at home, and because of the friends I had outside of school I really felt like a could be a really good friend.

But I had no confidence in relationships because lots of people were horrible to me, partly to do with my appearance, so I guess that was really a big deal in terms of how I viewed myself. People who didn't know me would take the piss out of me when they saw me, and that meant that I was convinced that I was really ugly. I think it wasn't hard to believe that the kind of person I was going to like would never like me back.

That was probably why I never dared getting into a relationship with anyone I liked because I kind of knew in my head that they wouldn't want to be with me, so they would just have made a mistake, and then they'd realise it, and then I would get really upset.

I had a really bad and very low self-confidence in terms of relationships with other people. I had brilliant friends, so I felt absolutely that I could be loved as a friend, but I totally felt I wasn't lovable as a partner, and so I only ever went out with people I didn't really care about, and they were all people that I was never going to be bothered if they split up with me because I wasn't that into them.

Those relationships weren't all terrible and there were some really nice bits, but they were very unequal relationships because I never let myself be vulnerable in that way. So, I never used to let myself be vulnerable in relationships. This was the first time I got into a relationship with someone who I genuinely really wanted to be with. That was because I was so completely vulnerable already.

I thought I couldn't make myself more vulnerable by getting into a relationship with someone I liked. This was the first time that I let myself be with someone I really wanted to be with, and it was extraordinary! It felt absolutely incredible because it was terrifying as I was letting myself feel everything, and I had never done that.

In the past, if everyone who I'd liked made a move on me, I instantly went off them because I loved unrequited love. There were loads of people I was passionately in love with over the years, so I would spend years being really in love with someone from a distance, and I would get to be a really good friend of them, and I would tell myself that it was totally unrequited. As a much older adult, I look back, and I can see actually lots of them did like me; but at the point at which they made a move on me, I went off them and stopped anything from happening and then made myself forget about that bit and then still thought that they didn't like me.

So, I only went out with people that didn't matter to me. The good experience was being with this person and letting it be an equal thing where we were both really invested in the relationship, and that also made sex much better. I don't know whether it's interesting or not, but I have always found it really easy to have multiple orgasms even if I had sex with someone I am not very much into, and that might be because I did masturbate a lot as a teenager. It kind of feels a bit bizarre saying it now. But I would never have told anyone I did it and felt really ashamed of it, and really embarrassed of it.

And yet, it really felt like an overwhelming need. I remember reading books as a teenager -we were all reading the same books in the attic, books we were reading at school- and these books did things to your inside that felt so bizarre and amazing at the same time. I wasn't having any kind of sex with anyone, and I wasn't having any kind of relationships with anyone else, so perhaps that is why I was masturbating more. Maybe you get much better at sex if you're doing it with yourself and then with someone else, so perhaps by the time I started to have sex, I was having more orgasms.

Tell us more about what felt good in this relationship.

I never felt pressure about having vaginal sex with him, and I wanted it much quicker than he was up for it. It was the first time I ever had had oral sex, and also the first time I had given a blowjob because I hated the thought of it so much. I had been with someone for several years, and I knew I would never ever be able to give him a blowjob because I found it so utterly repulsive.

And then, when I was with this other person, he thought it was such a normal thing and that it was normal to talk about it, and so for him, he felt very strongly that you wouldn't have sex before you would have oral sex.

For me, I always found oral sex much more intimate than vaginal sex, so it felt the wrong way round! But I didn't feel pressured into it -it felt odd to me, but he was never trying to push it.

However, for him, we wouldn't have had vaginal sex before we had oral sex, and that was both ways. He felt that vaginal sex was a really special thing and that you would want to work up to it over a while, whereas I would have had vaginal sex with him pretty much the day I met him, but nothing on earth would have made me have oral sex with him straight away because I find that much more intimate than vaginal sex. Because it's in your face, and your face is so personal! And it doesn't mean that vaginal sex is not personal, but in some ways, I think kissing can be as intimate as having vaginal sex because your face is a very personal thing. Anyway, he was very kind and gentle and understanding, and we talked lots about a lot of things, and the sex was amazing.

Summary

- The impact of bullyism on young people
- Lack of self-confidence
- Being vulnerable in a relationship
- Sexual reciprocity
- Masturbation
- Different sexual acts

Points for Reflection

1. What counts as bullyism?
2. Why do some young people bully other young people?
3. What is the best defense against bullyism?

4. Can lack of confidence impact the types of relationships we choose?

5. What does it mean to be vulnerable in a relationship in terms of feelings?

6. Is there a specific age by which you should feel confident enough to have a 'vulnerable relationship'?

7. What is sexual reciprocity? What are the advantages of reciprocity?

8. How can you explore what reciprocity looks like for you and your partner?

9. What is masturbation?

10. Is masturbation more frequent in a particular gender?

11. What can be the benefits of masturbating?

What was the worst sexual experience you had as a teenager?

There was this friend of mine, who was really nice. I went to visit him once. He used to live in a small studio where he also used to work, which meant that we were sitting on the bed because that was his place, and that was the only place to sit in his room. We got drunk, and so pretty much straight away, we were in bed.

Now, this is someone who is genuinely really lovely, but I guess he was also inexperienced or even a virgin at the time. He was surprised, I think, that we got together, and so was I, and we didn't have full sex, but I realised straight away, as soon as we were kissing, that I didn't want this. I didn't want to do anything physically with him at all, but I felt that it would be rude to stop, which made me feel like a prostitute.

I was there, hating myself for allowing him to do things to me that I absolutely didn't want. And he was so nice that if I'd said "I don't want this", he would have absolutely stopped. But I didn't have the confidence, and because he was so inexperienced, he didn't have an understanding of how things would go:

I wasn't pushing him away, but if you are inexperienced, you might not be aware of what it should be like, which is a two-way thing. I was being really passive, and if we both had known what a consensual act was, we would have known that that was not consensual. And so, it was only a minor thing.

We didn't have full sex, but it made me feel really lousy about myself for not having had the guts to say, "Actually, I don't want this", and I hated myself for it. And I resented him too, although he really didn't know and he was even younger than me. He just didn't get it.

Later, where it did feel much more unpleasant, I had a boyfriend who -and I think this probably happens to a lot of young women these days- if I was sitting down, he might just come up and take down his trousers and pants, so his penis was right near my face, expecting me to give him a blowjob, and I thought it was disgusting.

But I went along with it, at least some of the times. I have such a very different view on all of that now, and I would be much more comfortable to just putting a stop to what I don't want to do.

I think, clearly, he thought that was completely an acceptable part of being in a relationship and that he could, from nowhere, with a kind of sexual arrogance (we could be having a conversation about something, or we might have been eating at the table), drop his trousers because in his head he was getting kind of sexually excited and he had an erection, so he could just present me with an erect penis and expect me to want to put it in my mouth.

You will never catch me doing something like this, ever.

Of course, I didn't see that and thought, "This is what a good relationship looks like", but I did absolutely feel pressure to do it because, and it's because of this terrible Englishness about being polite and not wanting to embarrass someone else, and not having enough self-worth to say "This doesn't feel nice".

So, there's an expectation of politeness, and it's the same feeling that you get sometimes when you're walking down the street feeling uncomfortable about someone walking behind you, but you don't want to 'make a scene', so you won't call someone out on something.

There have been times where I haven't crossed the road when I felt uncomfortable because I didn't want to make the other person feel bad if their intentions weren't what I was concerned they were.

And it's that same lack of self-worth, I think, lots and lots of girls and lots of women have, where they think that other people are more important and come first. And, again, I am actively trying to overrule that now and I am much better at that now.

Summary

- Consent

- Lack of self-worth and confidence

- Being 'active' and being 'passive'

- Holding responsibility for one's own safety and pleasure

- Holding responsibility for your partner's safety and pleasure

- Politeness and putting other people's feelings first

Points for Reflection

1. What is consent, and what does it look like?

2. Who is responsible to express and ask for consent during a sexual act?

3. Can someone change their mind about consenting to sex during the sex taking place?

4. What can they do about it?

5. How should their partner react?

6. Are people supposed to be 'active' or 'passive' during sex according to their gender identity?

7. Is there one gender who is not entitled to withdraw consent?

8. Is there one gender that naturally always consent to sex because they just always want sex?

9. How important is it to express or advocate for yourself?

10. Is it possible that if we don't prioritise our needs, then other people will also not prioritise them?

11. Is it possible to healthily love others if we don't love ourselves?

12. What's politeness got to do with it?

13. What does 'being kind to oneself' mean?

Carol's Insights

I think that, first of all, if you treated yourself like you treat your friends, you'd be in a much better position. I treated my friends really kindly, I was really nice to them, I could give them really good advice, I was really good at listening to their problems, and I treated them with respect, which I never treated myself with. I had such a low opinion of myself, and if I could, I think I would go back and tell myself not to worry about what other people thought of me.

I think because I was bullied, what other people thought of me was extremely important because I was hearing it all the time. I think

I would tell myself that that was about the bullies and not about me -well, it was a bit about me, but it's alright to be different. So, yes, to treat myself like I would treat my best friend would have been sound advice.

Also (and I'm not talking about taking risks that are dangerous), but I was so scared about taking risks on people that I liked that I would rather stay safe and single than let myself find out what it might have been with someone that I liked. I was also petrified of making mistakes - and I think this is a really big thing. I was so scared of making mistakes that I never allowed myself to take any risks, and that included going out with people that I liked. I was so terrified of looking stupid because that's part of how people commented a lot on my looks when I was younger.

So, I didn't do things I wanted to do, and I think people should be less concerned about making mistakes and more accepting that actually making mistakes is a fantastic way to grow. You forgive other people for their mistakes constantly, and it's not really forgiveness because there's nothing to forgive. You might think, "Oh, he tried it, and it didn't work!" and that's fine, whereas, again, I would have never been that kind to myself, and I missed out on so many things that could have been really nice, including potentially really nice relationship.

In terms of sexuality, I think people are in a much better position now, certainly in the UK, about sexuality. But it's the same thing about taking risks. If you are never going to be the one to make the first move, it's like a Venn Diagram: if you think of the people that you like and the people that might like you, and then if you're never going to ask anyone out, you have a little overlap and you're only going to get the chance to be with the people who are prepared to ask you out.

And if you never ask anyone, if you are never prepared to be the one to initiate something then you are excluding so many possibilities. There are people who, if you went out and approached, might absolutely be up for something happening, but if you don't, then you're only going to get a certain kind of person who is going to approach you anyway, so you are massively shrinking your pool of possibilities.

And that seems crazy. And I have to admit that at my age, in my 40s, I have still never made the first move on anyone, and I think it's a really shameful thing. I still think it's terrifying, but who knows, I might one day, and I hope I will.

And about sexuality, I have only ever been out with men, whereas I'm attracted to men and women, and because I've never made the first move, I haven't created an environment where that's more likely to happen, which means that I have massively excluded people.

So, I've had a whole life of never being with a woman, whereas probably 30% of people I like are women, and it just seems crazy. I think people are in a much better position now to just go with whatever, and I think sometimes you do need to be more proactive, especially in that respect.

When we were growing up, there was an absolute assumption that people were heterosexual, and so unless you were a little bit more forthcoming about it or a little bit more obviously open to the possibility, it was unlikely that you would get together with someone of the same sex.

I could go my whole life and have partners that are just men because it's easier, and I will never have experienced going out with a woman. So, the advice is: know yourself, be true to yourself, have integrity. Be kind to other people, but also make sure you are as kind to yourself as you are to other people because it's very easy to be kind to other people and a whole lot harder to be kind to yourself.

Summary

- Loving and being kind to oneself
- Fear of getting it wrong
- Taking the initiative

Points for Reflection

1. What does 'being kind to oneself' look like?

2. Is it harder to be kind to oneself than to others in your opinion?

3. What does 'being brave' mean to you?

4. Is it brave not to let other people down but to let yourself down?

5. What are the benefits to except that you are bound to make mistakes in relationships? Or to have grace towards ourselves?

6. Are there still social expectations on who should take the initiative in asking one out for a date?

7. How do you feel about taking the initiative?

Your Notes and Critical Thoughts

Chapter 4
Story of an Abortion

Charley, 54, England

What was the best sexual experience of your adolescence?

My best sexual experience and relationship was probably with Dennis, my first boyfriend. He was a real gentleman. I got together with him when I was 16, and I absolutely adored him. I put him on a pedestal, and there were a lot of dates before we had sex.

But thinking about it, which I have, I did feel pressured to have sex with him in a way, and I remember him feeling frustrated, and I remember him saying, "I want you! I want you!" and I remember telling my mum about that, and she was quite empathic.

I remember her going, "Mmh…" but she didn't offer any advice, and I don't know if my mum at that time was assuming that I wouldn't give in. But I remember him also saying to me, kind of brushing myself off, "Gosh, you make it sound like you are a conquest! I remember thinking, "Well, I don't quite know what's all that about..." I knew it was derogative, though, and that he was putting pressure on me.

Nevertheless, eventually, we did start having active sex on a regular basis, and it was good. I enjoyed it. He was my first; I lost my virginity to him, and prior to that, I only had some little interactions, as you do. However, some of them felt a bit dirty because obviously they weren't the right person. But we didn't use protection, and that was absolutely folly, certainly on his part, because I must have been 18 or 19 when I got pregnant, but he was a lot older than me, he was 22 or 23. He had already gotten a girl pregnant and had a son from a previous relationship. She was a very devoted catholic girl and had gone ahead with the pregnancy, which I obviously didn't -to my mum's horror.

Looking back, we had already had a teenage marriage with a baby in our family, as my cousin fell pregnant at around that age. Her family was in the process of emigrating to America, and they found out when they got there that she was pregnant. So, they took steps to let her come back to the UK, and initially, she was going to marry that boy, but then it didn't happen.

He decided it wasn't for him. They were going to get the baby girl adopted when she would have been born, but they couldn't go through with it. She's an author now; she writes great books in the States, and I don't know if she's ever made contact with Dave, the dad.

But to go back to my point, my mum knew I was pregnant, but she didn't say anything. She didn't think I would take the steps to go and have a termination off my own back. I had no support, went and did it all on my own, and my mum was absolutely horrified because she would have actually embraced a grandchild even though I was really too young, and it wouldn't have been right for me. Looking back, I think my mum would have been quite happy to have brought that child up alongside the family.

But I was having none of that. I was very aware at that age that that would have completely changed my life to the point that I thought, "Well, I don't want to be a married teenager!" And also, at that point, I can't remember the timeline well, but I can't remember how I felt about Dennis at the time. I mean… I loved him, but I think I started to change the way I felt about him and I think I didn't know if I even wanted to be with him long term.

And do you know what? In all honesty, I can't remember how he reacted to the news. I think he was supportive, and I think, if anything, he would have probably wanted me to go ahead and have the baby, but I don't have any memory of that. I was just so focused on what I needed to do. I've always had this reputation in the family of being the person who "cleans up her own shit", and I'm still like that now! So that's really what I did: I had messed up, and I needed to sort it out.

So, what made sex with Dennis good?

Because I loved him, I adored him. I was in love with him and I think that's what it was. It was like he couldn't do anything wrong at that particular point. I think we were in a strong relationship, and if I'm honest, I genuinely think that we loved each other. My downfall with him was when I woke up and started to see him for what he really was. You know, when someone is on a pedestal, it's like they can do no wrong. He was like Adonis to me, and then suddenly, the chips in the armour had started to appear.

And one night, he got really drunk on New Year's Eve, and he accused me of flirting with his friend. His friend Steve wasn't quite an oil painting, quite the opposite, and I had never fancied him in any way, shape or form. Anyway, coming home from the party on New Year's Eve, Dennis lost his temper.

I had used my salary to buy him a Raymond Ray watch, which was expensive, considering wages at the time. So, he had this beautiful watch that I had bought him for Christmas, but then he took it off, and it was snowy.

There was a lot of ice and gritting sand on the road. He got himself in such a strop that he tore the watch off and threw it in the gritting sand. I then dutifully went to recuperate, saying, "Oh, no! The Raymond Ray watch that I bought you for Christmas!" So, I retrieved it and obviously saved it, but that was a turning point in our relationship because it's a sad and horrible thing, but there's no way back (there never is) when you've lost respect for someone.

And it just went like that! And from that moment it was just little steps. And I had met someone else that had caught my eye. He started to criticise the current Dennis… so I started to look at him in a completely different light, and it went downhill from then. We split up.

I am not proud of having an abortion by any stretch.

The only thing that I'd do differently is using contraception, you know. I can't believe, looking back, how my mum didn't choose to take control. Bear in mind she was on her own with me and my two sisters, and that didn't help. And I think that my mum probably thought, and I only learned this many years later, that this could have been some sort of a tool for my dad to come back. Maybe she thought that things could be turned around, you know?

I don't really know what was going on in my mum's head, really. So, I'm not proud of what happened, but I don't beat myself up about it either because I was probably not educated in that department as much as I needed to be. I think I was naïve, but I don't blame myself because I was 16. It was just really unfortunate…and why did that happen to me? I don't know. I can only say that he probably took advantage. I think he should have been far more careful, especially because he had already gotten pregnant somebody else, do you know what I mean?

There are different things here at play: I don't blame entirely myself, and I think it was a catalogue of different things that played. I don't blame my mum, but I think she could have been a lot more proactive about making sure that we were using contraception. I think Dennis's mum got wind of what was going on before my mum did because the letter from the hospital. I deliberately got it sent at his address, so she picked up on it, and she actually said to her son, "You should have known better! What on Earth were you thinking?" And he should have taken more responsibility for that than he actually did!

Summary

- The responsibility of contraception
- Lack of sex education from parents
- Dealing with an unwanted pregnancy
- Having an abortion
- Moving on from a mistake

Points for Reflection

1. Whose responsibility is it to sort out contraception?
2. What would you do if you got pregnant or if you got a girl pregnant?
3. How could you support your girlfriend at this time?

4. Who would you ask advice to?

5. Who gets to decide about having an abortion or going ahead with the pregnancy, giving birth to a baby, opting for adoption or becoming a parent for life?

6. Is there one right way to feel about getting pregnant?

7. Is it important to allow yourself to move on from having had an abortion?

8. What is the best way to move on? How can you make sure to avoid putting yourself in the same situation again?

9. Can the Internet be a good educational resource?

10. Does porn show people talking about or using contraception before engaging in sexual acts? If not, why is that?

11. Where can young people get effective and realistic sex education on contraception if they do not get it from their parent? Please share your resources with your peers.

Points for Deeper Reflection

1. How do you think it feels like being pregnant or knowing you got your girlfriend pregnant?

2. In which ways can an unwanted pregnancy affect the single individuals? And the couple?

3. Is it important to be kind to yourself during the entire process of deciding what is best for you as a person?

4. Can different people have different feelings about going ahead with an abortion?

5. Is it OK to feel serene and peaceful with yourself about having an abortion?

What was the worst sexual experience of your adolescence?

Make sure you find someone who really respects you, who loves you because I made a mistake with one particular guy where he was a player, a total player. He had numerous girlfriends, and I don't doubt that I was probably one of his favourites, but there were many other favourites. I was like Tuesday girl, and he had Friday night girl, Saturday night girl and Sunday morning girl. We rarely spent the night together. So, I think it's really important to have someone who respects you and respects your boundaries. I can't really think about anything that I would want more than that, really, and also for the feeling to be mutual.

Somebody once said this to me: "Do you want to be with someone you adore, or do you want to be adored?" and I have never been quite able to work it out. It's such a conundrum because there are pros and cons: I don't want to be feeling like "I love you but not as much as you love me". I want equality, actually, because it's really important to have that in a relationship. But I think in reality often one loves slightly more than the other one, and I can't answer which one I would want to be. And I think it's really important that your partner respects you, respects your boundaries, cherishes you and loves you for you.

Summary

- Being with a 'player' and being a 'player'
- Setting up boundaries and expecting respect
- Equality in a relationship
- Romantic feelings and balance in a relationship

Points for Reflection

1. What is a 'player'?

2. Is a 'player' a particular gender?

3. Would it bother you if your partner had sex with other people?

4. Is it a good idea for people who have sex together to have a conversation about whether they want to be exclusive or not?

5. What are healthy boundaries in a relationship?

6. What are 'double standards'? Are they healthy?

7. Why is being in an equal relationship healthy?

Point for Deeper Reflection

1. People are different and like different things, but as long as they are honest with their partner about what they want in a relationship, then they should be free to do what they want. What do you think about this statement?

Charlie's Insights

Make sure you use contraception unless you are quite prepared to go through facing an unwanted pregnancy -and I don't know how anybody would want that. I think probably in my days, and certainly the background I came from, sexual education wasn't prioritised in the way it should have been. I am not portioning blame. I'm just stating how it was, what happened and why. I think that today, contraception is a lot more available.

My mum came from the generation where sex before marriage was a no-no, and of course, the pill came along. And that's when we had the Sexual Revolution because it meant that women didn't have to get married in order to have sex because that's how it used to be.

So, my parents came from a northern, almost backwoods sort of attitude. And, of course, STDs are something to be aware of, so using contraception not just from a contraceptive point of view.

And I have a friend who drinks, and she literally lets the reins go, whereas when I drink, I always make sure that I can get myself in a taxi and I can get myself home, and I like to think that I've never made myself too vulnerable, which I think it's very easily done. This is really something you have to be aware of. I think someone put something in my drink when I was in Australia once and attempted to rape me, but it didn't happen. But you have to be self-aware, you owe it to yourself and to everybody else to be responsible for yourself.

You make sure you don't drink too much, and you get yourself in a state where you don't know what you are doing or what is happening around you. And taking drugs comes under the same umbrella as drinking, doesn't it? Even if you are a big girl, the moment you make yourself unconscious, you are vulnerable to massive risks. Never let someone else take the reins because that's when you are vulnerable.

Also, when you are out, don't go off anywhere on your own; always tell someone where you're going and go to the toilets with a friend. It's silly little things, it's common sense most of the times, but you can't always teach that. So, it's something you always practice or something you learn through bad experiences.

Summary

- Sexual and Relationship Education
- Sexually Transmitted Diseases (STDs)
- Being self-aware and in control

- Making yourself vulnerable to risk
- Sexual assault and blame

Points for Reflection

1. Are parents responsible for educating their children about contraception?

2. Is the school responsible?

3. What STDs do you know?

4. What are the physical effects of being drunk or high?

5. What are the undesired effects?

6. What risks would you make yourself vulnerable to if you were drunk or high to the point of not controlling your movements?

7. Whose responsibility is it to keep yourself safe?

8. How important is it to watch over your friends, too?

9. No matter how drunk or high they get, a person is never to blame for being sexually attacked by someone. What do you think about this statement?

10. If someone gets drunk, and then they get sexually assaulted, are they partly to blame?

11. Does wanting to be drunk or high mean wanting to be sexually assaulted?

12. Who is guilty when someone drunk, or high, or not in control of themselves gets sexually assaulted?

13. What would you do if you were sexually assaulted? Who would you talk to?

14. What could you do to help someone if they told you they had been sexually assaulted?

Points for Deeper Reflection

1. What is 'victim blaming'?

2. Should a survivor of sexual violence feel ashamed or like they are to blame?

3. Who should feel ashamed and take the blame?

Your Notes and Critical Thoughts

Chapter 5
Recognising Rape

Charlotte, 32, Spain

*WARNING: Sexual Assault Themes

What was the worst sexual experience of your adolescence?

The worst experience in my adolescence has bizarrely only been identified as such by me in my mid-20s. I must have been 18 or 19 back then, and I started to be friends with a guy who must have been around 24 or 25. I wasn't in love with him or anything like that. In fact, I was in love with another young man, Sergio, who unfortunately didn't correspond to me.

In truth, I was completely heartbroken over Sergio, and I carried on feeling like that for years. However, I knew that probably nothing would ever happen with him, so I started trying to date other people. The guy I'm talking about didn't seem romantically interested in me.

However, I kind of got an interest in him because he was an older guy; he appeared to be different somehow and seemed to have a bit of a complex personality. He was what could be defined as an 'outsider'. I couldn't quite figure him out, and I guess that made me feel curious about him. It is also true that teenagers tend to validate themselves according to the validation they get from other people or according to their ability to 'conquer' people they fancy, which is quite natural. So, in retrospect, I probably saw him a little bit like a challenge and wanted him to like me.

We started going out for walks, the cinema, mini trips out the city and a couple of times we had drinks in the evening. I can't remember how long we hung out together, but during the whole time, he had never hinted that he was interested in me in a romantic way or even in a sexual way.

Therefore, I guess I felt pretty safe with him, although I hadn't known him for a long time. Once, we went out for drinks with another couple of friends to celebrate someone's graduation, and I got really drunk. I guess everyone was drinking, but perhaps I ended up being more drunk than the rest of the group.

Anyway, we ended up crashing at this couple's flat. As soon as we got there, the couple went upstairs to the bedroom, and me and this guy stayed in the living room. I don't remember very well what happened for a while but what I can remember is that he literally jumped on me out of the blue.

I remember I was drunk because I wasn't coordinating my limbs very well, and I didn't have much balance. I don't even remember how undressed I was or how he got me undressed. I remember feeling a lot of pain. I remember that his penis felt like steel in my body, and it hurt me in every movement he was doing. I remember saying the whole time, "No! Stop it! You're hurting me! Stop! Listen!" over and over and over.

The entire time. He never stopped and never said a word to me. He just continued doing what he was doing in the same way as one would do some vigorous physical exercise. I was very confused the whole time about why he never listened to me or never responded, and about how he would do something to me without acknowledging me talking to him, my pleading to him, like I wasn't even there, like I wasn't talking. I remember that when he finished, I was very relieved, but I also felt like crying. But I didn't.

I didn't cry. I never cried. The next morning, I don't remember when he left or how I got back home. I felt angry at myself, and I remember thinking, "So you wanted something to happen with him, didn't you? Now you've had it, something did happen with him." I never thought for a moment that I had been raped.

In fact, I didn't know I had been raped. I had seen a movie when I was younger called "The Accused", and I thought that rape only looked like the one featured in the rape scene -which was literally horrific. That's all I knew about rape. I didn't feel that I was entitled to complain about anything or report to anyone because I had wanted some kind of romance to sparkle between us, so it was nobody's fault if I had not happened to like his approach, his way. He never did seek my company after, and I certainly didn't call him again. The fascination I had had for him obviously disappeared completely after that night. I never told what happened to anyone for nearly 2 decades.

It took me all those years to realise that even someone you like can rape you. Even someone you love or are crazy about can rape you. Just like, I suppose, even a husband can rape his wife or his partner, and the fact that they are married does not make the violation, the violence, the pain go away.

And that's why it's illegal, even if it is your spouse the one raping you. I understood after all those years that I had been raped, even if by someone with whom I had hoped for something special to happen. I never saw him again for years. Until I met him in a supermarket almost 2 decades after, after I realised what had happened.

I remember he was walking with a friend, and I was there with my daughter, who was about 12. I felt so agitated and panicked. When he walked past me, he said hi and said something like, "Oh, you are still very beautiful!" It all happened so quick, and I didn't want him anywhere near us. I didn't get the clarity to say anything to him.

When I thought about it minutes later, I said in my head all the things that I would have wanted to tell him, like, "Oh, and do you still go around raping drunk friends?" or "You big piece of shit, don't think for a moment you can talk to me!" But I didn't. It's one of my biggest regrets.

Summary

- Growing up and self-validation
- Rape
- Reporting rape

Points for Reflection

1. Do young people tend to validate themselves according to who they get to date? Why?
2. What constitutes as rape?
3. Can people with male genitalia be raped or sexually assaulted?
4. Is sexual assault or rape as traumatising for them as for people with female genitalia, or who are intersex?
5. Is there a hierarchy of gravity according to who the victim is?
6. What is consent, and what does it sound like?

7. Can it be hard to stand up for oneself during a sexual violence?

8. If anything like that happened to you, who would you talk to and why?

What was the best sexual experience of your adolescence?

I had the best love story with my first-ever boyfriend. He was my first kiss and my first time. I really fancied from the moment I saw him, and he fancied me too. I was 14 when we met. I remember clearly feeling incredibly attracted to him. He was handsome, had big dark brown eyes and a sexy accent from Rome, which distinguished him from all the boys I knew and who treated me with contempt because they thought I was different.

He was alien to all those silly little games because he had come from a different town, so he didn't see in me what the others saw. I suppose he saw me with brand-new lenses. Anyway, we got together and I remember the first kiss we had -which felt a lot more wet than I had ever imagined. Though, by that time, I was super ready to have my first kiss. I had dreamed about it for such a long time and I only ever wanted to kiss him. I even remember the first time I touched him between the legs, and I never expected the penis to become so long. Let's just say I had not gotten any sex ed at home or in school, so there you go. Actual anatomy ended up being a surprise.

We were crazy about each other. We loved each other and deeply cared for each other. Our love was very romantic, all-consuming and passionate. We shared the same taste in music, and we were inseparable. He used to make me drive his Vespa, which I found super-hot, and he used to buy me lovely presents with his pocket money. And we could not get our hands off each other.

We had our first time together, although I don't remember it being a one-night enterprise, but rather penetration seemed to happen a few centimetres deeper at each time -in fact, I had started doubting I also had a 'whole' like other girls. If only my friends had explained that I needed to have plenty of foreplay to start off to enable me to feel horny and to allow my vagina to become lubricated!

And sure, we never spoke about consent back in those days, but our being together was totally organic. I would clearly show my desire to have sex with him with my entire body and my hands, mirroring his body, his hands and his desire, and we would be focused on reading each other.

I love that I had my first sexual experience with someone that I loved so much and who loved me back, who had the highest respect for me, and who was totally concerned with our happiness and our mutual pleasure. You might wonder how I could get it so wrong in recognising rape after such a lovely relationship. The reason is that I had a very difficult upbringing. I had no one to go to, and I had no one to talk to about my problems or my confusion. And I never had any form of sex ed.

Summary

- The first time
- Pleasure
- Being in love
- Being loved

Points for Reflection

1. What is the first time? Is it the same for heterosexual and LGBTQ+ individuals?

2. Do people necessarily need to be in love in order to feel pleasure during sex?

3. Do people need to feel respected in order to feel pleasure during sex?

4. How does it feel to be in love?

5. How does it feel to be loved by a partner?

Charlotte's insights

Well, clearly, I want everyone to be very clear about what constitutes as sexual assault, which is anything sexual that is done to you when you don't consent, but even when you freeze, when you can't move and push someone away, or you are unable to speak, when you are quiet the whole time, and you can't even say no, or when you have your eyes closed the whole time because you are scared or you are crying.

And I want people to be clear about what consent is. Don't listen to those who say, "Oh, asking and consenting step-by-step is such a buzz killer! How does a guy make the first move these days?"

That is totally ignorant and shows a lack of creativity. First of all, if your partner is not expressing their desire in their body mirroring yours, seeking physical contact, seeking your body, then they are probably not as into whatever is happening as you are -and the question here is if you care about their pleasure and desire. There is no buzz-killer in asking your partner questions like:

- Do you want to do this?
- Do you want to have sex with me?
- Do you like me doing … or …?
- Would you like to do … to me?
- I would love to do … to you. Can I?
- Can we try to…?
- What would you like me to do to you?

Asking these types of questions is so mature and actually grown-up, and it can feel anything from cute to downright sexy! It is a statement of mutual respect, and all the while, it can be very hot as well, so a totally win-win situation!

There really is no excuse for not being aware of how your partner feels, and there is no longer room for misunderstanding on both sides. This means both parties have the responsibility to let their partner know if they are into what is happening or not, as well as to make sure they are aware if their partner is into what is happening. It goes both ways and so consent should be in a relationship or sexual intercourse where there is mutual respect and absolute equality. And also, if it's not there, it's a crime!

Summary

- Consent
- Buzz-killer
- Asking permission
- Taking responsibility for oneself

Points for Reflection

1. What is the difference between rape and sexual assault?
2. Do you think asking questions is a good way to ensure your partner is consenting to sex?
3. What can constitute as a buzz-killer, in your opinion?

4. Is it OK to try to do something sexual to your partner without asking them permission first?

5. Is it important to take responsibility for your answers or what you express you want to do sexually?

6. Can you blame your partner of sexually assaulting you if you say you want to do something that you don't?

7. Can people change their minds about doing something even if they have already said they would do it, or they have done it before with that same partner, or they are in the middle of doing it?

8. If your partner says they consent, but during sex, they do not move, do not speak and do not look like they have any pleasure, would you be worried? Would you continue doing what you are doing anyway?

Your Notes and Critical Thoughts

Chapter 6
Psycho-Physical Maturity and Managing Doubts

Hanna, 26, England

What was the best sexual experience in your adolescence?

Yes, so when I was 19 or 18, I got together with someone for six years. I did think he was a good guy, but when we started to see each other, I didn't really want to get into a relationship. I was quite naïve at that time. However, from the start, he really wanted me to be his girlfriend, and I was just like, "Oh, it doesn't have to be very serious…". But he really wanted me to be his girlfriend, so that was cool. Also, what made him special is that he didn't put any pressure on me to go much further in terms of our sexual relationship than I felt comfortable with, and he didn't at all, ever actually, put any pressure on me.

I was with him six years. We started seeing each other in September, and we didn't have sex until May. I kind of led really all of that. I mean, we used to make out and things like that, but it was just a very slow development, and so… yeah, I kind of led that in the end, which actually was a bit difficult for me at times because we both were virgins, so we didn't know what we were doing and it was a bit like the blind leading the blind.

I always felt that I had to initiate things and I found that frustrating, and I felt that it was a bit strange. But then, in later years, I realised I probably shouldn't have felt like that because it is quite nice to be in control, to be completely comfortable. I hadn't had any sexual partners before and only kissed a few people because I was quite naïve. And being quite old, you know, I was 19 when I lost my virginity, I wasn't really that confident, I suppose, physically, and I wasn't used to tap into my sexuality because I just was probably quite shy.

Sex was good, I suppose, because I was really ready for it, and half of me was really desperate for him to take the lead. I was really ready for that to happen, and, yeah, the first time we actually had sex, I think it was a little bit of a failure. In all honesty, things happened for him that he wasn't really expecting, shall we say? But then we tried again and it was fine, and yeah, we didn't stop!

Honestly, I still treasure him as a person and I know how special he was, so compassionate towards me. Because we'd been together for so long, six years, he had been my only partner. There came a point when I wanted to explore more, and because he wasn't so forthright, I actually wanted to have other experiences, which obviously I have had since. But that didn't devalue what we had had, and in subsequent experiences, I realised how kind and tender he was and how that's the true value of love and sex for me.

Summary

- Taking the initiative
- Psycho-physical maturity
- First penetrative sex
- Early ejaculation
- Being connected to your partner

Points for Reflection

1. What does 'taking the initiative' mean?

2. Should a particular gender take the initiative?

3. How do people know they are ready to have sex, in your opinion?

4. Are there benefits in waiting to be ready to have sex?

5. How likely is it for the first sexual penetrative experience to meet expectations?

6. Is it common for a boy to ejaculate after a few minutes during an early penetrative experience?

7. Is that something to be embarrassed about?

8. Is it OK to make them feel bad about it?

9. Are there any strategies that can be put in place to facilitate female orgasm taking place? What are they?

What was the worst sexual experience after him?

I have had a couple of bad experiences. I suppose the worst was when I was with someone, and he made me feel like aspects of my physique weren't what he would have necessarily wanted. I subsequently realised that he had quite an overexposure to porn, and this influenced the way he behaved with me sexually. He never did anything without my consent, so I've never been in that situation.

However, certainly, I think that he wanted to have a particular excitement level which he felt that I wasn't really giving. I'm quite a strong character, so it was like, "Well, sorry, you know, I don't want to get into some kind of argument about how good I am in bed and how good you are in bed" because I didn't feel like that was appropriate, but now I know that this is something you should be able to have a healthy dialogue about, what they like and what you like, and things like that. That should be an open conversation and people should try to kind of dance around each other. But with him, it wasn't like that.

For example, he would prefer a woman who had no hair at all, and it's not like I have a lot of pubic hair, and I personally prefer to have some pubic hair, and I think that's part of how I feel about myself and my identity of being a woman. And that's important to me. I have at different times taken all my hair off, but I didn't really like it because I felt like I was a child because the last time I had my vulva looking like that, I was a child! So, I was like, "OK, I understand that's your preference…" But then he was like, "Oh, you know, I've even had to start watching porn that has women with more hair and more housewife stuff so that I can kind of get into this a bit." and I was like "OK, good luck with that then, crack on!" You know?

And I didn't really mind that he was watching porn, but when he was bringing that into our relationship, I was like, "OK, this is strange." He would also say things like, "Oh, we have to always have sex on your terms!" And this is interesting, actually. I never really thought of this before, but I was saying about my first partner not wanting to lead sex, whereas with this guy, he would say that sex was always on my terms.

And, actually, we used to have quite a lot of sex, but there were times when I had been working, and I don't remember ever refusing to have sex with him because I actually really like having sex. But it was just a little bit too much, and I suppose we just didn't connect! But I think that what you realise when you get older is that there are so many other aspects that come into your sexual life.

When you're young, you just want to have sex all the time, but when you are older, other things come into play, like how much you are able to see each other and just general day-to-day logistics of what you're doing, which don't make it possible to just spend all day in bed. It's just different.

Anyway, those were the sorts of things that he was saying to me. He also used to tell me how I wasn't really that great giving blow-jobs, but many people since have told me that I'm quite good at that. And I was like, "Well, what would you like me to do?" and he would say, "You need to do it like this! Or you need to do it like that!" But he would not say it in a way that was kind of encouraging, like when a man's touching you and you're like, "OK, this feels nice!" but he was like "You're not doing this right! You need to do that!" and I was like "Really?! OK, do you want to just do it yourself?"

There are all different kind of reasons why you are with someone, and we didn't split up because of sex. It wasn't that. I don't think it's just as clear-cut as that. I have had partners that, even though we're not together, if I had the opportunity, I would still have sex with them again. But with him, no.

Summary
- Porn-led expectations
- Feeling entitled
- Communicating about sex preferences
- Being true to who you are and how you identify
- Standing up for yourself

Points for Reflection

1. Do you think that sex represented in porn is a veritable depiction of real-life sex?

2. Can watching porn warp your idea about what sex is and about what you and your partner should behave like during sex?

3. Can watching porn warp your understanding about what is likely to feel nice and what is unlikely to feel nice in terms of pleasure and safety?

4. Is it OK to expect your partner to groom their body the same way porn actors do?

5. Is it OK to expect your partner to perform sexually in a particular way?

6. Is sex about performance? Or what is it about?

7. How can one express their sexual preferences in a respectful and considerate manner?

8. Is putting pressure on your partner to do something they are not comfortable doing sexy?

9. How do you imagine that may feel if you were at the receiving end?

10. When someone feels under pressure and criticized, are they likely to also feel sexually aroused?

11. Can acting in an entitled way actually put your partner off from having sex with you?

12. What sentences could you say to clearly express you do not want to do something during a sex?

13. What sentences could you say to clearly express doing something in a different way does not feel good to you during a sex?

14. Why is it important you express clearly what feels good and what doesn't?

15. Is it easy to guess what people like or don't like?

16. Whose responsibility is it to ensure all parties are into what is happening?

Hanna's Insights

If I were going to give anyone any advice, and also to my younger self (and to myself now), I would say that sometimes you get yourself into a situation where you feel compromised, and you don't really feel that comfortable. And if, for whatever reason, you don't feel that you can do something, you can actually stop that situation because there can be all sorts of emotional and psychological things that make you feel like that. Make sure that you give yourself space to think about it, and don't put yourself in the same situation again straight away. Just sit back and take stock.

You can think, "Right, that wasn't that pleasant. That wasn't what I wanted, but I'm not going to let that happen to me again!" and be clear about that. Accept that these things can sometimes happen, and sometimes people have bad experiences in all sorts of different ways, not only sexually but psychologically too, like people blackmailing you. And especially in intimate relationships, be really honest with yourself and try to make sure you don't repeat it. Have a conversation with yourself. Basically, at some point, give yourself that space and don't repeat that behaviour.

Summary

- Feeling compromised or uncomfortable
- Taking time to reflect
- Being true to who you are

Points for Reflection

1. What could make people feel compromised or uncomfortable during any sexual activity?
2. What could they do in any such situation to stop?
3. Is it likely for young people to find all the right answers to their questions fast?

4. As a young person, is it possible to feel confused about what one likes or not, or the type of sexual acts they want to try or do, or not? Why?

5. Is it useful to take time to reflect and to understand ourselves?

6. What's worse: letting other people down or letting yourself down?

7. Who is responsible to show other people how they should treat you?

8. Is it realistic to expect people to be able to read your mind and know what you want and what you like?

Your Notes and Critical Thoughts

Chapter 7
Equal Sexual Expectations

Helena, 40, England

What has been the best sexual experience of your adolescence?

The best sexual experience of my adolescence has probably been one I had at around the age of 19. I don't remember how we got together exactly, but I remember that he was very much into me. I think he was also slightly younger than me; he was probably 18. He was very handsome and tall, and he had lovely dark eyes. I was not as involved with him as he was with me because I felt I was a little more mature than him.

Also, I was depressed at the time, so I felt like he could not really understand me and what I was going through. However, he cared for me a lot and always put my needs high on his list, or at least he tried. Because of his naivety, he was also carefree and fun, which is something I craved to be around a lot in those days.

He was from a perfect, wealthy family, and I wasn't, and my family was nowhere near as normal and put together as his. And that was another reason why I thought he had no idea about my struggles, and deep inside, I thought he could never understand. But he was there for me as he could be, and he would show up for me the way he knew how.

So even sex was nice with him because he would make me feel important and valued, and he actually adored me. I liked sex with him, although I never had an orgasm with him, nor with any other boy.

At that time, the topic of female orgasm was oddly ignored by literally everyone -girls, boys, parents, friends, the whole world! And oddly enough, boys would come, but never, ever ask, "Have you come?" Which is, anyway, a ridiculous question because female orgasm is quite evident; you can't not hear it! But my point is that they would not even ask, and us girls would not mention it nor expect it the same way boys expected theirs. Part of it was a complete lack of sex education at school and at home, but part of it was that our culture was insanely patriarchal and misogynist, and nobody even was conscious of that! Anyway, he was adorable, and I have a fond memory of him! I'd like to say hi to him after all these years, but sadly, he's not on social media, at least under his name and surname, so I guess it won't happen.

Summary

- Being different but caring

- Being 'selfish in bed'

- Sexual expectations and Self-awareness

- Sexual education and awareness of others

Points for Reflection

1. Is it possible for two people coming from a very different background to be in a relationship and effectively care for one another?

2. What does 'being selfish' in bed mean?

3. Would you be able to draw the entire anatomy of the clitoris?

4. In your understanding, where is the clitoris located? At the front or at the end of the vaginal canal?

5. Is it realistic expecting to have an orgasm even without having knowledge of the anatomy and location of your clitoris and of how it works?

6. Is it realistic expecting to enable your sexual partner to have an orgasm even without having knowledge of the anatomy and location of their clitoris and of how it works?

What was the worst sexual experience of your adolescence?

The worst experience was with a man that was a lot older than me, like 25, and I was probably 18. That experience is really the one that I would love to erase forever. He was a sly, dirty man, but he was a friend of a guy that I was desperately in love with who did not love me back. So, I went with this man because I wanted to make the guy I loved jealous... how silly of me! I did not enjoy anything in that encounter. There was nothing nice about it, no connection whatsoever. I clearly was not thinking straight, and I was very, very immature.

So much so that I did not even use contraception and ended up getting vaginal warts off him. He was a promiscuous man, and I should have known better. In fact, I did know he was promiscuous, so why did I let myself down like that? So many times, I have thought to myself, "What was I thinking???"

But I have managed to forgive myself, and I have tried to understand why I did it. Sure, I could continue loathing myself and believing that I deserved whatever I got as a consequence of acting so irresponsibly, but that did not feel fair. I would not be so harsh or judgemental of a close friend if they made the same mistake, so why would I be so harsh towards myself?

Certainly, that turned out to be a massive learning curve, but at the same time, I had the right to forgive myself and move on. And I did it because I was very confused about who I was. I was so obsessed with that other guy that I never asked myself why I loved him or if obsessing over him made me feel good about myself. He was not on the same page as me, and yet I was crazy about him (and I acted out of desperation!)

I never asked myself what I loved about him, how did he make me feel and if those feelings (anxiety, obsession and willingness to be his doormat) were worthy of pursuing. I never asked myself why I wanted him so desperately, or what could actually make me happy, what values I had for myself and in a relationship, or what qualities I was looking for in a boyfriend.

Summary

- Not thinking straight
- Rejection
- Learning curves
- The right to be wrong
- Reflecting
- Self-forgiveness
- Doing what's best for us

Points for Reflection

1. What does 'not thinking clearly' mean?
2. Has it ever happened to you not to be thinking clearly?

3. Do you think Helena dealt with being rejected well and healthily?

4. Do you think it is difficult for young people to deal with rejection? If so, why?

5. Do young people feel generally equpipped to deal with rejection?

6. Do you think that often when a young person is rejected by a person they like, they may attach their inner value to that?

7. What do you think constitutes a person's value?

8. How common is, statistically speaking, that someone will be rejected by someone they like?

9. How common is, statistically speaking, that you will reject someone that fancies you, but you do not fancy?

10. What does it mean when someone's romantic interested is not mutual? Is it personal or is it chemistry? Or is it just statistics?

11. What do you think Helena learned from this experience?

12. What does 'love' feel like? What does 'sexual attraction' feel like? Are they the same?

13. Is it possible to have a positive sexual experience with someone purely on the ground of sexual attraction?

14. What are the basis for that to happen whilst preventing someone getting hurt?

15. Being an adolescent, are you likely to make mistakes?

16. How useful is it to take stock of the causes and consequences of our actions?

17. What is self-forgiveness?

Points for Deeper Reflection

1. Are you ever kinder to your friends but not to yourself? Why? And is it right?

2. Identifying the reasons behind our actions can be useful. What questions would you ask yourself (or a friend) when deciding to have or not to have sex with someone?

Helena's Insights

Well, I want to say that all teenagers in the history of time made mistakes. They made mistakes, they are making mistakes, and they will make mistakes. That comes with the territory. You are growing, your brain is still growing, and stuff happens. Gosh! Even adults make mistakes! Some do more, some do less and we should all aim at self-improving. If you have also made a mistake, what I want you to do is understand why you did it.

Then forgive yourself and move on because you have the right to be wrong. Nobody is perfect! Learn your lesson, and turn the page. In fact, Einstein said that the definition of madness is doing the same thing in the same way and expecting to have different results, which I think it means you can treasure what you have learned from your experience and find a better way.

Another important thing is challenging yourself in understanding what motivates you to engage in any kind of sexual act with someone. For instance, you could ask yourself:

- Do I really want to do this?
- Why do I want to do this?
- Are the reasons good for me?
- Am I respecting my values and who I am?
- Am I sacrificing something I believe in in order to do this?
- Am I doing this for me or for someone else?
- Would I advise my own best friend do this?
- Does this person make me feel safe?
- Does this person make me feel respected and valued?
- Do they care enough about me?
- Do I care enough about them?

You'd be surprised how useful this is, especially if you write it down. It's something I've learned through experience, good and bad, and I swear by it. You have to try to do what is right for you because taking care of yourself is one of the most important things you will ever do -and obviously, that doesn't mean you disregard other people's needs and feelings.

And think about STDs. Ok, if you get one, it is not literally the end of the world, and some STDs like chlamydia, gonorrhoea, syphilis or genital warts can easily be treated and cured. So, if you have had sex without protection, you should not have sex with someone else or wait to have symptoms -you should get tested.

We're so lucky in the UK, it's free and easy to find a centre. But there are diseases way more serious, such as HIV, and you can live with it, but it will have an impact on your entire life. Are you prepared to go through that just because you can't be bothered to plan to have a condom, to wear a condom or because you can't refuse to have sex without a condom?

For one moment, think about a condom and using it. It literally takes nothing, a few seconds. It takes minimal effort compared to the fun and freedom to enjoy sex. It takes self-respect and respect for others, and an appreciation for your health and your partner's. Well, in all fairness, it takes maturity, and perhaps if you aren't mature enough to be responsible, it's because you are still a child, so you shouldn't have sex. I'm not trying to be paternalistic. Or preachy. I'm being as honest as I can because I believe that sex is great and is fun, but like anything else we do in life, it takes ~~some~~ learning, maturity and practice.

Summary

- Contraception and STDs

- Sexual health centres

- Condoms

- Responsibility and sex

Points for Reflection

1. Do you know if other contraceptive methods also protect from STDs apart from the condom?

2. How long does it take to wear a condom?

3. Can you name a single sexual health centre in your city?

4. Do you agree with Helena that if you can't be responsible, it means you are still a child and should not have sex? If so, why?

5. What does 'being responsible enough to have sex' look like to you?

Your Notes and Critical Thoughts

Chapter 8
Adolescence, Religion and Sex

Katarzyna, 35, Poland

What was the best sexual experience in your adolescence?

I actually didn't have any boyfriend until I was about 16. He was someone that I knew from primary school, and when we moved to secondary school, he kind of reappeared on the scene and then someone told me that he had really liked me for the whole time. It was obvious that he fancied me. But then we had our first kiss, and I always say that scarred me for life, in fact, I don't like kissing because of my first kiss.

Obviously, looking from this perspective, after all these years, I know that kind of kiss is more intimate, it wasn't just a kiss on the lips, it was what they call a French kiss with tongues straight away; it was just horrible! He was a very nice person, he never did anything I didn't want to do, but his style of kissing was horrible. He wasn't doing anything wrong, and he didn't want to hurt me or push anything on me; it kind of happened quite naturally, but I had not expected it to be that way. I hadn't expected that there were tongues involved. Just a second before he did, I knew he would kiss me… but it was horrible because it was so wet, and I still remember that our teeth touched. Oh, it was really bad!

I don't remember what my expectations were, but I think at that time in my life, I never thought about the practicalities and technicalities of kissing. Perhaps for me it was all about lips than anything else. In my times and because of the religion I was unfortunately brought up in Poland, which is a Catholic country, there was a very certain picture of relationships and stuff, and because it was so many years ago and in a very religious country, sexuality obviously wasn't talked about.

And also no one would ever tell you things like that, and we were not really interested in going beyond or talking about the first kiss. But I definitely remember the feeling and I didn't like it, and it put me off kissing pretty much for life. It wasn't until 2012 when I finally met a man I enjoyed kissing, but I was already in my late thirties.

Was this a positive experience?

Well, yes and no. I wasn't really ready for a relationship. I liked him, but I didn't like him in the same way he liked me, and I got in the relationship because of guilt. It was the first time that someone was really showing a lot of interest in me, and I never considered myself a pretty girl. I always considered myself fat, and because I used to go to the same school where my mother taught, obviously, I was a known person, and I got bullied because of this and that. I had my own issues.

As I would say, I was never slim. So suddenly, someone was showing an interest and he was a very nice guy, and instead of involving my heart as well, I decided exclusively with my head. And I remember the guys I knew they were always gentlemen, so they would actually ask if you wanted to go out and if you wanted to be their girlfriend; and as a girl, you would always wait to be asked.

So, we started seeing each other a little bit, and I felt that he probably really wanted to be my boyfriend. We got to the moment where he asked me, "Do you want to go out with me? Do you want to be my girlfriend?" and I'll never forget that I opened my mouth to say 'no' but 'yes' came out instead. And I shocked myself because it was like, "What the hell just happened?" And I felt so guilty and so embarrassed I could not bring myself to say, "Sorry, I meant no." So, that is why I started seeing him.

But in terms of sex, we never got there. I think I kind of blame the religion, so for me, it was how I was brought up, not by my family because they weren't that involved, but by the church. We would go to religious lessons, and basically, as a woman, I remember I was constantly getting the message that whatever I would do, it's my fault.

So, for example, if you put some make-up on, you're a *whore*, if you have a slit in your skirt so it's easier to walk, you are a *whore* because 'why don't you just split it open and show your ass.' Basically, those were the messages that I was getting, and 'God forbid' you had sex with anyone because then you were a total *whore,* and everything was your fault, right?

So, for me, it was mostly about holding hands, then he would try to embrace me, and that was fine. I knew he would want to go further; after all, we're talking about a 17-year-old's hormones. But I always thought, "On my God, but if I do this, then I'm going to be a *whore*!" There was always that guilt and the thought, "This is forbidden!" So, he would try to touch my breasts, as you do, but everything was on the clothes, not under. And I didn't let him do too much. We only had one moment when he was on top of me, and he was trying to get under my skirt, but he never went higher than my knee or my thigh because I would tell him, "Oh my God, what are you doing? This is wrong!" and stuff like that. But he never pressured me into anything, and one time, I remember his nose started bleeding.

He was embarrassed because he felt he was too horny, and that had happened because of his hormones. So, he said, "It's OK, nothing's happened! Nothing's happened!" I think he was scared that he had crossed the boundaries. So, I reassured him, but I wasn't feeling good and not because of what he had done, but because I didn't want to be a bad person and a *whore*. And I had my urges, too, and I recognised that it would be nice to be touched and be naked, but I never ever could.

At that point, did you start fancying him and desiring him?

No. I mean... I had some urges, but I don't know if I fancied him. I had my fantasies and used to think, "OK, so he's a good person, and maybe I should marry him, and this is just the way it is" But, again, that was because of the constant messages I was getting that I shouldn't want too much: if the guy is good, that's enough if he is going to look after me, and if he has a house or his parents are going to build him a house and blah-blah-blah, then we should marry. I liked him as a person but there wasn't a physical attraction. But as he was lying on top of me, that is probably when I started feeling some kind of pleasure, but I thought, "Oh my God, no! I don't want to do that!"

The point is that I should have never said yes in the first place. I ended up in that relationship just because I felt guilty and embarrassed.

Summary

- Lack of self-worth
- Settling for anyone
- First kiss expectations

- Gendered behaviours and expectations

- Religion and gendered sexual shame

- Sexual urges and desire

- Fear of being rude

- Prioritising other people's feelings

Points for Reflection

1. Can feeling unattractive influence someone to feel unworthy?

2. Can feeling unattractive influence someone to get in a relationship just because they've been asked?

3. Do young people have expectations about what sex or even a kiss should feel like?

4. Expectations can be unmet or exceeded: what are the crucial factors for an enriching experience?

5. According to some religions, sex should only happen between married people. What do you think about that?

6. According to some religions, sex before marriage is dirty and wrong. How do you feel about that?

7. Some religions tend to put a lot of shame and guilt on women for being sexual people, but not on men. Are there historical reasons for that? And do you think they still apply in modern societies?

8. Are there cultural reasons for these double standards? Are they fair and supportive of gender equality?

9. Is feeling sexually attracted to people part of human experience regardless of your gender? Why?

10. Is it possible though not being sexually attracted to others?

11. Do you know what it means to be 'asexual'?

12. For heterosexual people, is it usually up to boys to ask girls out? If so, why? And are these cultural behaviors attuned to a society grounded on gender equality?

13. Is it ever a good idea accepting to be with someone or to engage in sexual activity just for the sake of being polite or fear of upsetting someone?

*WARNING: Suicidal Feelings' Themes

Is there any other sexual relationship that has had an impact on you as a young woman, positively or negatively?

Yes. So, because of the earlier experience, I always thought that me and men don't mix, but then I had what I call my first serious boyfriend. I was around 25 years old. That was a sexual relationship, although, again, we never had full sexual intercourse. But I remember observing myself going through the whole process where I kissed him. We were at a small house gathering and we were having fun, talking, drinking wine, and playing games.

And he had been giving me signals for a very long time, so when I was a bit tipsy, I felt brave enough to kiss him -just the lips, nothing to do with tongues because that was horrendous for me. And I thought, "OK, that wasn't too bad, that was acceptable!" That's when kissing became acceptable; it didn't give me this gag feeling I had felt with my first boyfriend.

We started having more sexual experiences very slowly; he would put no pressure on me whatsoever. He would try to do things, but he would always check on my reactions. I think I was very lucky with my boyfriends in this sense. He was the first guy who put my hand on his private parts, and I was surprised, but I didn't want that.

I was like in my early twenties, and I still couldn't go all the way because of this frigging catholic belief that I'd be a *whore* and it's dirty. Sometimes he would try to have a conversation to understand what was going on because we were together for 2 and a half years, and we never had full vaginal sex. We tried, but it was very painful, so he would never ever worsen things.

But he was worried that I didn't want to have sex, and I would have to explain to him that it was because of my religious guilt. I really didn't believe in God at that point, I wasn't really following any religion, but the catholic guilt was still there because I thought that everyone would always look at me as a *whore,* whatever I did physically. I fell in love with him, and he was the first person to whom I said, "I love you". We wanted to get married and have kids.

What happened then?

I thought I loved him, but looking back, with experience the understanding of love is different compared to when you're younger. The problem was that he was a very negative person, and he wasn't in a very good state of mind. I was studying to be a social worker, and I thought I could help him - you know how sometimes a girl just wants to help the guy. He showed me some of his old poems, which were extremely dark and suggested he had been contemplating killing himself. He did change his outlook a little bit, and through our relationship, he seemed to be feeling more positively as there was a lot of love.

However, what happened was that I soaked up his negativity, and my friends started noticing how much I had changed from being a positive person to appearing quite down to perhaps his level. One time, my best friend had a go at me because I was making stupid comments to the kids we were working with. She was really mad, and I remember running home crying and having a panic attack. He was there helping me, but I soon realised that I had needed that reality check from her, and I realised what was happening to me, whereas his spin on this was that I should not mix with people who were upsetting me.

But I knew in my heart she was right. I reflected and started noticing that every time he was away, I'd feel a lot better, and friends would make comments about me, seeming like the 'good old me', but when he would be around, I'd feel a shift to the worse in myself.

So, one time, he was talking about getting married and having kids. I had a clear vision of being dead within five years if I had gone down that road -I would have probably killed myself.

When we broke up, we would sometimes speak on the phone to talk things through, but sometimes he would say that if he had had a gun, he would have killed himself. And I remember thinking, "You don't get to blackmail me. If you try to blackmail me, that's fucking it". And even if I was aware of his history, I felt like, "No, don't put your shit on me. If you decide to kill yourself, that's on you!"

Summary

- Carrying religious guilt
- Respecting people's boundaries
- Toxic relationships
- Wanting to 'save' your partner
- Emotional blackmail

Points for Reflection

1. Can religious or sexual guilt be overcome?
2. Is it important to respect other people's boundaries?
3. What is a 'toxic relationship'?

4. How could being in a toxic relationship impact on your life?

5. Is it plausible to think we can help someone who is depressed and suicidal?

6. What could we do to help a partner (or a friend) who feels as low as the man in the story?

7. What is emotional blackmail?

8. If someone you know was emotionally blackmailing you, would you know where to ask for advice and guidance?

9. Can you be responsible for someone else's life?

10. If someone you know told you they were feeling suicidal, would you know where to ask for advice and guidance?

Katarzyna's Insights

I have learned a lot. I learned to follow my gut. I should have finished with that guy much earlier, but I never had the strength to do it. I waited and waited until once another guy and I kissed, which made me understand just how much I was not happy in my current relationship. Instead, I was always blaming myself and holding on.

So, always follow your gut feeling and don't allow anyone to put you under any pressure. For instance, the first time I had sex, I was putting pressure on myself because of my distorted perception of English guys and thinking this is what they 'expected' of me. I had a warped prejudice on what English men were compared to

Polish men, so I started to have sex basically because that was what one would do in this country.

Did you enjoy any of these sexual encounters, or did you feel you were only doing what was expected of you?

I think both because, in terms of sexual pleasure, I'm pretty good at this. Even if I was doing it to meet expectations, I was with a guy who cared for me and, treasured me and cared about my pleasure. I've had my pleasure. Although once, trying to build him up, I said it had been better than the actual reality. But I still carried the burden of the catholic teaching inside.

When we did it the first time, I went to the bath tab, and I was shaking and crying, terrified. And he cared for me, asked me what was wrong, worried he had hurt me. I told him that I was scared he would leave me now because he would think of me as a *whore.* That's why I'm talking about pressure from inside: pressure to have sex as expected and pressure of being judged as a *whore.* It's important to question your perception of yourself and deal with *what is in front of you,* and not constantly fearing the judgment in your head.

Communication is everything, and don't rush into anything, especially when you are in your teens, because there is a lack of maturity and understanding of what sex entails and what a relationship is. And, as an older woman, I would say you need to have confidence in yourself and have your head screwed on to be able to deal with difficult situations, like distinguishing between something worthy and emotional blackmail.

If you ever are under that kind of pressure from a guy moaning at you, demanding, "Give me a blowjob if you love me" remember that demanding has got nothing to do with love and all to do with wanting pleasure from you. And I'd love for young people to be able to identify blackmail and to not give in to it.

Also, being an adult has nothing to do with having sexual experience. You have to have emotional and physical awareness to be an adult. More sexual experience and what your peers think of you don't make you mature any faster. You can live without sex, really, when you think about it.

Summary
- "Following your guts"
- Putting pressure on yourself
- 'Building someone up'
- Judgment
- Emotional manipulation
- Maturity

Points for Reflection

1. What does "following your guts" mean to you? Why is it an important ability to have?

2. Is putting pressure on oneself less damaging than peer pressure?

3. What does 'building someone up' mean?

4. Should anyone lie to make their partner feel good?

5. Is there an expectation for boys to be better lovers than other boys?

6. Is it a girl responsibility to make her boyfriend feel they are the best lover they have had, and vice versa?

7. Do young women experience the same pressure to be good lovers?

8. In your opinion, is there a difference in these expectations according to gender? If so, how does it relate to gender stereotypes?

9. Can gender stereotypes be harmful? If so, how?

10. What makes a person a good lover in your opinion?

11. Do you think many young people fear the way others judge them?

12. Do you think many young people can be harsh when judging themselves?

13. What is 'emotional manipulation'?

14. Is it okay to manipulate your partner to convince them to do something they don't want to do?

15. How can you spot if you are being emotionally manipulated?

16. What does it mean to be an adult?

Points for Deeper Reflection

1. Is there a difference between being encouraging to your partner and building their confidence, and feeling obliged to 'massage their ego' by exaggerating about the sex experienced with them?

2. How can one find a balanced way to live without fearing other people's judgment?

Your Notes and Critical Thoughts

Chapter 9
Standing Up for Yourself

Laura, 41, Italy

What was the worst sexual experience of your adolescence?

The worst experience was with a boy who was a little bit older than me and who was the brother of a classmate of mine. I thought I liked him, and I accepted his invite to be with him because I fancied him and he was genuinely a good-looking guy. However, as we got to a certain point, I realised that that was not what I wanted, and I felt his hands on my body in a way that made me feel uncomfortable.

Thankfully, this episode wasn't too traumatic because, fortunately, I stopped myself on time, realising that that wasn't what I desired. I am happy that I was able to recognise my needs and stopped the experience before it concluded itself in a way that I would not have wanted. Therefore, yes, it was a negative experience because of his way of touching me, which I remember being a little bit as you would expect a maniac to touch you. What I can say is that I hadn't expected it to be like that.

Summary

- Taking control

- Standing up for yourself

Points for Reflection

1. Is it likely for someone to change their mind once they realise what they are doing isn't what they thought it would be like?

2. What does 'taking control' in an uncomfortable situation feel like?

3. How does 'standing up for yourself' makes you feel?

What was the best sexual experience of your adolescence?

I believe that the best experience, strangely enough, was actually with the guy I had vaginal sex for the first time. He was completely in love with me, but I realised I was less in love with him, or perhaps I wasn't in love at all. I remember that I decided to do it with him, as it happens for most girls in those years, because of my curiosity rather than actual sexual desire, and honestly, I didn't want to be one of those girls who hadn't done it yet.

The experience was great. Sex with him felt amazing, a little bit like the movies, full of romance, with candles lit all around at his house when the parents had gone out. In that way he was a very sensitive and attentive kind of guy. It felt truly wonderful and I have beautiful memories, and not so much for the physical pleasure of it as the first time can be rather painful. It would be untrue on my behalf to say that it was fantastic in terms of sexual pleasure. But on the emotional side, it was absolutely wonderful. He was very handsome, and I liked him physically, but he was very much in love with me, so much so that after we did it the first time, he bought me a ring the next day.

That is the reason why I finished it with him because I knew that, in reality, I had wanted to have sex with him just to satisfy my curiosity more than anything else. But at least I really have lovely memories of my first time.

What made it special was the way he treated me, and the way he touched me because I could see that he really cared about me. After that episode, however, he kept coming to my house wanting to speak to me or even my parents because he wanted to marry me, which made me feel rather anxious, and in the end, it made me want to put an end to it all.

After all, I was a young girl, I was 16, and he must've been 19, as he had a car. However, I felt too young to get officially engaged as he would've wanted.

Summary

- Reasons to be with someone
- Feeling rushed into adult decisions
- Prioritising yourself

Points for Reflection

1. Is it possible that two people go into a relationship or have sex for different reasons?

2. Are there 'good reasons' or 'bad reasons' for wanting to have sex?

3. How can people avoid being misunderstood by their partner?

4. Is being honest with our partner about our motivations the right thing to do? And how can it be done?

5. Is it common to feel rushed into making adult decisions?

6. Nobody is going to prioritise your interests if you don't. What do you think of this statement?

Laura's Insights

My advice would be that, as long as you are being honest and respectful of your sexual partner, do what you like without fear of any type of judgement. If you want to try to have an experience with men or with women, do it. I believe that everyone is free to try whatever they want to try. In fact, the advice that I would've given myself back then would be to be less repressed. I could have experienced more. I could have let go of my inhibition a lot more, whereas often, for fear of being judged I limited myself. I haven't had many experiences that I wish I had.

I think that perhaps, though, the right time for this is when you're in your twenties. For instance, only late in life, I have realised I am bisexual. In fact, I currently live with a woman, and I wish I had tried to be with a woman a lot earlier in life. I'd say to my younger self: "Don't limit yourself to men! Don't necessarily wait to get to the age of 30 to do what you desire." I'd say: "Be yourself."

Also, I hate labels. And I am convinced that labels should only be on clothes. Even if I were a lesbian, I wouldn't be comfortable with the idea of being labelled a lesbian because I think that we are what we are in that specific moment. I like people, I like a person.

If they are a man or a woman, or something in between, it doesn't really matter to me. I could like a man, or I could like a woman, or I could like someone who is transgender. For instance, I currently live with a woman and it has been ~~three~~ 3 and a half years now. But this could all be over at some point in 1, 10, or 20 years, and I could happen to fall in love with a man. I just don't know, but it's OK.

Summary

- Being yourself

- Fear

- Labels

Points for Reflection

1. Is it okay to take your time to work out your sexual preferences?

2. What is the difference between being fearful and being responsible?

3. What are the labels Laura is referring to, and what do you think of them?

Points for Deeper Reflection

1. Some people feel comforted by being able to identify with a 'label'; others feel that labels can feel restrictive. What do you think about that?

Your Notes and Critical Thoughts

Chapter 10
Insecurity and Peer-Pressure

Nadine, 54, England

What was the worst sexual experience in your adolescence?

I'll start by saying that I felt kind of insecure about my appearance when I was a young person, and I find I was sort of a late bloomer. I was awkward at 13, 14, very tall and not very confident. I had an older sister and a friend who was a year older, and she was very confident and very sexualised, I suppose, so I always felt like the awkward friend, that I was falling short and that I would have to behave in a certain way to fit in.

So, I think, firstly, this comes down to who you are, your confidence, your self-esteem, knowing where your boundaries lie because my first experiences were born out of trying to be liked, to be accepted, to fit in the "What, you have never let a boy do this to you?" or "What, you have not let him do that to you?"

You know. And sometimes these girls put you in situations where they are not your friend... I had felt so pressurised by my friends to have sex. But, well, I look back at the relationships we had, and I can kind of half laugh about it now, but there's a part of me that is very wounded by the fact that I seemed to be failing as a teenager in my friends' eyes for not putting myself out there.

Also, because I had a Greek father and a Greek brother, in that culture, any sexualisation expression from a girl is shameful when you're growing up. It's like, "Don't wear that make-up, don't wear that short skirt, don't bring shame to this family!" So, I wasn't able to express myself spontaneously that way, and it all became this secret with my best friend, saying "Why are you not doing this?" Or "Why are you not doing that?"

I think the important thing is, and I hope that girls can think about that now, is that I remember being fumbled within an alley up the road on my way back from school because I felt like the boy wasn't going to like me unless I let him touch me. And then it got talked about the next day at school.

Then, I was really flat-chested, and still am, and I don't care, but, because I had allowed myself to be touched that way, it became something that was sort of thrown around and caused me to have massive insecurities about my body... and that carried on, for a long time.

But he became like a crush, and I ended up giving myself away where I let him touch me because I wanted him to like me. But then I felt shamed and then it didn't get me anywhere anyway! It's not like he fell in love with me! Later, he tried again when I was older, but then I was old enough to say no.

So, I had sort of encounters but not proper boyfriends. Then there was a boy who teased me a lot at school, and my first relationship was born out of a boy who used to tease me, and then we got off with each other. I just think that's quite interesting because he was horrible to me and I was horrible to him back, and I think often that's how boys and girls relate to each other. I thought he was the guy that everybody fancied. I thought he was the guy who was powerful and cool; you know, I probably fancied him from afar.

I thought it was a way to get attention rather than being invisible. I thought that's what girls did to make boys like them. What happened was that we were in an alley of the suburb, and we were kissing, and then, as my friend had told me that I should have let him touch me, I allowed him to touch me in my pants and put his fingers inside me.

Obviously, it was thrilling in a way… but then I felt just so awful afterwards because I felt so shamed. And then we went back to school (and this is what generally happens) it got discussed! And then you have to walk back to that classroom, and if you are not safe with somebody and you can't trust them, you just give people power! You give people power to humiliate you!

When I look back now, I think, "You, actually, were really horrible to me, and I ended up being your girlfriend and giving you my virginity!" And I look back and think that he was never good enough for me, but I think because of this whole sense of insecurity along the way, I put myself in that position.

It's crazy if think about it! Imagine a young girl's mind, with all the kind of insecurities that are already there as I felt that I didn't look right, and I wasn't pretty enough, and then I had done something, probably against my best judgement anyway, but I had done it because I wanted to be accepted. Then I thought that now that person knew something so intimate about me, and he had probably told his friends because they didn't really care about me. And I had to walk back to an environment that was very negative for me. And what do you do then? You have to cut yourself down emotionally, somewhere, to be able to survive the day, survive the week, survive your life.

And I think you desensitise yourself to it, so you have to push it away, and I think that's what girls often do. I didn't become strong and confident for a long, long time, and I just gave little pieces of myself along the way. And that's why I say that I wish I had held back until my second relationship, because that's when I really became strong, and I knew who I was, and I had grown, and the sexuality had grown. Before that, it was all very much related to shame and pressure.

And nowadays I don't so much think about that boy, but I think a lot about that girl, the girl that I was…about that child…she's still with me. And it's not that I carry the insecurity now, although I did for a long time, but I wish she'd been more looked after if you know what I mean. I mean, there was a lot going on in my own life with family, and there was an opportunity for that girl to be a little 'adrift'. Looking back, maybe that's how it happened. So, I don't think about the boy necessarily, I think about that girl, that kid. And, I can't deny that I did feel thrilled as I did fancy him, you know.

We had an experience, and it was an awakening, there's no doubt about that. But in terms of whether it was worth it, I don't think it was. I would have probably been much cooler, and it would have made me better, in his opinion, if I had been cool for the next two years and held off. And maybe I would have then been able to get off with him after knowing more about his personality, or not. In a way, when you have done that in a rush, for the wrong reasons and with someone superficial who is only collecting girls, it's just like, "She's done!" Do you know what I mean? And I think kids need to be aware of that. Sometimes it's cooler if you don't!

Summary

- Feeling unattractive and insecure
- Feeling ashamed
- Peer-pressure

- Traditional cultures and attitude towards young girls
- 'Putting yourself out there'
- Trying to 'not being invisible'
- The cliché about boys teasing girls they like
- Being sexually available to be liked
- 'Giving' and 'taking' someone's virginity
- Shaming your sexual partner by breaking their trust
- Mental health

Points for Reflection

1. Is it uncommon to feel unattractive as a teenager?

2. Is it possible for teenagers feeling unattractive, and particularly heterosexual girls, tend to be more sexually available to make up for the fact that they think others don't find them attractive?

3. Can friends be the worst at applying peer pressure?

4. Why do you think some friends put pressure on their friends to be more sexually available?

5. Is it possible they might do that to justify or validate their own sexual behaviour or to feel more confident about themselves?

6. What does 'putting yourself out there' actually mean?

7. Should 'putting yourself out there' rather be about sexual desire?

8. Is it possible that if a teenager does not feel sexual desire it is because they are physically and mentally not ready for it?

9. What could be the consequences of such teenagers in forcing themselves to have sex?

10. Are there traditional cultures which are very oppressive of girls, but not so much boys? How do you feel about that?

11. Have you heard about the cliché that if a boy teases a girl, it is because he fancies her? What do you think about that?

12. Can this cliché be dangerous? If so, how?

13. What are more mature ways to show one you like them?

14. Do teenagers sometimes think that by being more sexually active, they will become more interesting or popular?

15. Is it true that some boys think they have to have a reputation of having been with many girls? If so, why?

16. Do sometimes boys apply peer pressure on other boys to boast about their sexual experience? If so, why?

17. If someone gives you more attention when you make yourself sexually available to them, do they like you or what they can get from you?

18. Is there any difference in the reputation of different genders being sexually active? If so, why?

19. Do you think it's right and coherent with gender equality?

20. Is it ever OK to gossip about people's body or about a sexual act involving them with the intent to humiliate or shame them publicly?

21. If someone talked to friends about intimate details of a sexual encounter with you, or of about your body, how would you feel?

22. What are the benefits of being intimate with someone you can trust?

23. How do you know you can trust someone? Does it take time?

24. Do you think that the notion of 'giving' or 'taking' someone's virginity may be outdated?

25. What could be the emotional consequences of pushing yourself to be more sexually active when it is not what you desire?

26. If, someone was talking about your body or about your sex life to others, what would you do?

27. If you were depressed or felt anxious following a similar situation, who would you talk to?

Points for Deeper Reflection

1. Do heterosexual girls think they have to be sexually available to make a boy like them? What could be the disadvantages of that behaviour?

2. Do boys think that too? If so, why?

What was the best sexual experience in your adolescence?

Well, it's been with the guy I had my second serious relationship with. We met at college and ended up getting married and having children together. He was a good friend, and then we grew in a sexual and loving relationship. We became inseparable. We would go to gigs together, travel together, go to festivals and have fun. We were also very supportive of each other and encouraging each other to do things and develop our talents. We both liked the arts, music and performing, and we did a lot of these things together and separately as well. We are not together anymore, but we are still friends. He was a big love, huge. And we've had an amazing adventure together and grown together, holding each other but allowing each other to be free and blossom, too. It was great.

Summary

- Friendship and love

- Holding each other and letting each other free

Points for Reflection

1. Is it possible to fall in love with your best friend?

2. What does 'holding each other and letting each other free' mean?

Nadine's Insights

I think sexuality is a slow-burner, and it's not just about being touched in certain awkward situations. People really think that you become sexualised because you start your period young, but you don't really start to understand about your sexuality until you are a woman. And so, it takes time!

And I think that there is a stigma about being a virgin within certain groups, saying, "I think I want to lose my virginity at 14, 15 or whatever". For what reason? It's going to be much better for you to wait for something that feels right, and you'll have more fun if you hold out and try to find a meaningful relationship. Then you'll feel fantastic.

There are other ways to explore your sexuality without putting yourself in danger: music can be very erotic, and reading can be really erotic, too. I believe that eroticism is something you can start within yourself instead of searching it all the time in others because often when you look back to those people and those friends, they don't matter to you any longer as they mattered to you then.

And you wouldn't take advice from them now. If you had the chance of having a snapshot of those voices back then, you know you shouldn't be listening to them! But I think, generally, because peer pressure is so huge at such a crucial age as 13, 14, 15, the need to fit in is more important than anything else, and that kind of blinds young people.

I think that your sexuality is something that shouldn't be affected by everybody else in your group: it's a very personal thing. I believe everyone should hold their sexuality and intimacy as a jewel, and I love it when I see young people that do that.

Treasure it and be proud of it because treasuring it is treasuring oneself. I am absolutely not saying that you should deny yourself something if you desire it; on the contrary, I am saying that you should not sell yourself cheap, and there is a big difference.

Summary

- Sexuality as a slow-burner
- The 'stigma' of virginity
- Eroticism

- Meaningful relationships

- Valuing your intimacy and sexuality

- Acting moved by sexual desire Vs 'selling yourself cheap'

Points for Reflection

1. What does 'sexuality is a slow-burner' mean?

2. Why is there a stigma in being a virgin? What do you think about it?

3. How do you define a relationship as 'meaningful'?

4. What are the benefits of valuing your intimacy and sexuality?

5. What are the benefits of engaging in sexual activity when moved by sexual desire that comes from within?

6. What does 'selling yourself cheap' mean?

7. Are there any advantages or disadvantages in doing that?

Point for Deeper Reflection

1. What is eroticism?

2. How can one explore individual eroticism?

Your Notes and Critical Thoughts

Chapter 11
Drugs, Sex and Blurred Memories

Roberta, 43, Spain

What was the worst sexual experience of your adolescence?

I've had plenty of negative experiences of a sexual nature when I was a teenager. However, the one that I remember being the worse it's probably when I had penetrative sex for the first time. I still feel quite saddened about it because I am aware there are some aspects that I still can't forgive myself about. I feel I did not give priority to my feelings, and I blindly trusted someone who wasn't able to perceive the part of me that was still childlike, so consequently I felt catapulted into a context that I don't remember positively, including because drugs were involved.

That's why I am unable to talk about the first experience as a pleasant one, because the drugs had altered my state of mind and feelings. Unfortunately, my first time was disturbed by the use of substances. I was 16 at the time, and he was 19, and he had already had different experiences in general.

I remember it as a negative experience because there was nothing poetic or romantic about it, and I didn't give the right importance to many aspects of myself. There was no care or love for that precious moment in itself, which could be perceived as the end of a stage of life and the beginning of a new one. I believe that there is more gravity attached to the first time you have sex than young people might think, because that is an experience that you will remember for the rest of your life, particularly if you gave it the right importance and you didn't diminish it. I surely wasn't giving myself the right value, so the person I had in front of me didn't give me the right value either.

In that moment, my mind was completely clouded, and I didn't have the clarity to put myself first and give myself value. This can happen more easily when one is fragile. When one is more centred and secure in their identity, they are unlikely to expose themselves in a similar situation. Fragile people have a tendency to see themselves through the eyes of other people instead of their own, and this is very wrong. It would have been crucial to take charge and to have a clear mind to be able to also say 'not like this'.

I also remember being impulsive, so there have been other negative experiences. Probably, I remember my first time as the worst because I would've liked to be able to say something different about it, but unfortunately, I am unable to. This was a bad experience because there wasn't enough love and care to frame that special moment of growing up, and I have been unable to honour myself and the importance of what it could have been.

I think about the trust I put in this person, and then I think about the value that this person gave me, which clearly wasn't enough. But it wasn't enough because I wasn't giving the appropriate value to myself, so I allowed it. I was too confused and distracted to align myself to who I was and what I wanted and to stand for it.

Summary

- Being high
- Putting your partner in charge of your physical and emotional safety
- Regretting

Points for Reflection

1. What does 'being high ' mean?
2. How can being high affect your judgment?
3. What are the risks of being high during sexual activity?
4. Are you more likely to regret doing something if you did it when you were high and so out of control?
5. Is it a good idea to put another person in charge of your safety?
6. Are other people responsible for your safety?

7. If you don't value yourself, others are less likely to do it either. Do you agree with this statement?

8. Do you also believe that the way a person makes love for the first time is as important as Roberta thinks?

9. If you did something you weren't proud of, would it be important to be able to forgive yourself?

10. What could help achieve that?

*WARNING: Sexual Violence Themes

One More Story

There had been another negative experience when I was 14, though, which I believe was probably closer to violence because I felt forced to do certain things. Once more, what led my experience was a lack of self-confidence, my curiosity and my great impulsivity. I was with someone that I fancied, but I found myself suddenly in a limited space with this person, suddenly knowing we were not on the same page. I remember he used to drive a motorbike, and I asked him to let me drive it as well.

But I asked him this in a friendly way, and not with the idea that I am a woman and I am asking you, man, a favour. There was no malice in my request, and I didn't have any second motivation. I asked him to teach me how to drive the motorbike, and he accepted, but before I knew, I found myself in a garage, alone with him, where he asked me to do things that I didn't want to do. I didn't want to be there, and I hadn't expected that pressure coming from him. I left absolutely disgusted because this person suddenly became aggressive and behaved like he was entitled access to my body.

Perhaps too often, when we think about violence, we somehow think about a gruesome scenario where someone hits you, smashes your head down, and you lay in a pool of blood, but violence isn't just that.

If a woman or anybody else feels pressured into doing something and unable to walk away, that is also violence, that is also traumatic because they are forced to act against their will. What I hated was feeling trapped because he had closed the garage gate. I didn't know what could've happened; things could've turned even worse. I've always been a person who liked the idea of being able to get up and go in any sticky situation, or whenever I pleased. So that experience was particularly difficult for me. I saw a side of him that I didn't expect, and he went from appearing kind to a state in which he didn't seem rational.

It clearly felt to me that the only thing that mattered to him was completing the sexual act. I believe I could've been anybody else because, in that moment, the way he saw me was simply like an object at his disposal. He also made me feel like I owed him something just because he had taught me to ride the bike, so I needed to give him something in return.

Outside the garage, other friends were hanging out, so when we got out of it, I also felt the eyes of everybody else on me because I imagined they knew that something had gone on between us. So, I also had to hear the little comments and got the little looks from the boys in that group, because obviously the girl is always the one that will come out worse, the one that will be thought of as a whore, the nasty girl, the easy girl.

Boys are never deemed responsible. Young men don't easily take responsibility for anything that happens; it is always the girls' responsibility not to do certain things, not go to certain places or even not to provoke the desire in a man.

I don't even know if he was aware of the pressure he put me under, and what my feelings were about it all. He certainly did not care to find out. I even had to pay the consequences of these events within my family because there were rumours about me and my behaviour, and one day my "dear" auntie and cousin took me on one side and ask me why I was visiting, if it was to spend time with my cousin or if it was to spend time with boys; —and clearly, what they meant was that I was a little whore.

I am sharing this story, and I am going on about it because I want to make a particular point which is the following: at the end of the day, no one asked me what had happened and how I was, and even people close to my family gave it for granted that the correct version was the one provided by strangers and dodgy boys. And this only added to my confusion and my feeling misunderstood and unimportant.

The most unexpected thing happened years after, when I was in my 20s and working in a bar. He came in and was very shocked to see me behind the bar, but the first thing he did was say he was sorry. I was astonished. But sexual desire should never obscure our minds and lead us to behave in disgusting ways. We are not animals and must educate ourselves.

With age, he must've gained a level of maturity enough to look back at what he had done and feel he had done me wrong. He said, "I am sorry, really I am", and I was trying to find the right way to react because on one hand I wanted to hit him in the head with a baseball bat, and on the other, I was surprised. So, I just looked at him and said, "Well, OK." I believe that teenage girls are different from teenage boys, and this is important to consider. Yes, we are impulsive, but at the same time, we are also more affectionate, so we go into a relationship more with our heart than with our body.

Summary

- Blaming oneself
- People that abuse
- Manipulation

- Consent
- Sexually objectifying a person
- Blame and reputation
- Being wrongly judged
- Accepting responsibility
- Truths or gender stereotypes?

Points for Reflection

1. Is being curious a positive or a negative quality per se?

2. Is being curious wrong? Is being impulsive wrong?

3. Has Roberta's personality at that time anything to do with what that young man did to her?

4. Do you think some people feel entitled to have sexual access to others?

5. If you found yourself in a similar situation, what could you do to stand up for yourself?

6. Is it okay to manipulate people in thinking they owe you and must repay you by performing a sexual act?

7. What is sexual violence?

8. If you experienced any form of sexual abuse or violence, who would you talk to?

9. What does 'sexually objectifying a person' mean? Who does that?

10. How does it feel to be sexually objectified in your opinion?

11. Is it still more likely for girls to be judge to 'be sexually easy' or are nowadays all genders considered equally?

12. Is it ever acceptable to blame someone who has been sexually assaulted for what has happened to them?

13. If someone you cared about judged negatively for being sexually active, would you want to set the record straight? What would you do?

14. Is it brave to accept responsibility for past wrongdoings, admit them and apologise?

15. If someone sexually assaulted you, would you be OK with receiving an apology, or would you report it to the police?

16. Boys mostly care about being with someone sexually, and girls mostly care about the emotional connection: is this statement true or is it just a gender stereotype dictated by culture?

What has been the best sexual experience of your adolescence?

I'm afraid that throughout my teenage years I haven't had pleasant experiences, so I will just talk about this one that I've had in my early 20s. This one felt wonderful because everything felt natural and with no pressure whatsoever. There were no lies, just the feelings that this person and I felt unconditionally towards each other. I felt that this was a visceral exchange, and this is probably because it felt we were able to look into each other's souls. So, the connection between our souls was also expressed through our bodies, and that is what made it so fantastic.

I would feel like one with this person, so it was never just a sexual act. It really felt like doing each other good through exploring every centimetre of our skin. I believe we often forget that the body is made of millions and millions of cells, so we don't have to always only focus on certain parts of our body. I believe this approach is probably only possible when individuals are mature, conscious, self-aware and aware of others, which is a slow process, undoubtedly. But it really is the best thing, because even a hug can be more wonderful than any sexual act.

It feels like you want to taste, you want to 'eat' the body of that person, because you feel at one with them. It's a beautiful feeling because it goes beyond a mere sexual urgency. And time flies, time disappears. And even if you try to recall everything that's happened, you can't. Time doesn't exist anymore, and it is amazing, almost like waking up from another dimension and saying to each other, "Oh my God, what's the time? It's super late!" I remember these times really fondly, for as long as they've lasted, because everything changes and even feelings transform.

But I love remembering about this person and about the time we've shared together, even if things have changed with time. I am free from any regrets and full of the most amazing memories, and full of love, not only for that person but also for the person I was in that moment, where there was soul and body, love and sex. And that is just the best way to be with someone, and it is rare.

Summary

- Being self-aware
- Being aware of your partner
- Body and soul

Points for Reflection

1. What does 'being self-aware mean?'
2. How can we become more self-aware?
3. What does 'being aware of others' mean?
4. How can we become more aware of our partner?
5. What does it mean to be with someone 'body and soul?'

Roberta's Insights

I would say to stay away from drugs, even though adolescents may not perceive the risks of using them at all. I personally felt like I wanted to experience so much, all at once. Therefore, it was problematic for me to feel and act rationally. When you use drugs, it is very hard to be in charge of yourself; actually, it's impossible. But often young people take them anyway because they don't love themselves enough, at that age. I clearly remember moments in my adolescence when I felt very paranoid and lacked in self-confidence. I did not feel strong enough or good-looking enough, and I was anxious about fitting in. In the case of the first experience I shared, for instance, that person should have done more (or less, actually), but most importantly, I should have been more responsible for myself.

I think that girls have certain expectations when they get closer to an older person, and certain psychological aspects are suddenly at play. On one level, they want to let go, and on the other, they are seeking some level of protection from someone who is often not able to protect them. The truth is that one should believe in oneself and never think of putting their life in the hands of another person, even though it is difficult at that age to think of these things in advance. Adolescence is a time when one is likely to make mistakes. Hormones are involved, and the longing and curiosity to discover a new world and to experience life can take over. So often, adolescents get involved in situations that are not reflective of who they really are and what they stand for.

There are many things I could say to someone beginning to have sex, but I'm afraid they wouldn't really listen. So, I advise to read, read as much as you can, because it can teach you so many things. And if you are uncertain and you don't know who to ask, find out for yourself, educate yourself. The best advice I can give you, though, is to get an education on drugs and to not try understanding them by trying them.

This is a very dangerous territory, take my word for it. Unfortunately, sex and drugs are often two aspects of life that teenagers feel curious about, and it really is a danger to mix them. Fragile people will try to take drugs to feel more confident and to appear cooler, because they need some help or support, but drugs will make things worse, eventually. And don't expect other people to look after you, even if they are older than you, because they won't.

You have to be responsible for yourself, you have to be conscientious towards yourself, to have integrity towards yourself and to hold on to your convictions. Don't try to fit in or adjust yourself to please others. Nowadays, more and more parents are trying to leave the door open for hard conversations. Of course, it is their responsibility to educate their children and to not leave them ignorant, and they should build their knowledge day by day, and not just leave their children to their own devices.

If you cannot get answers within the family, try to find them elsewhere. But don't be reckless, be smart about it. The Internet can be a great pool of resources to increase your knowledge, but don't be mistaken: the sex you see in porn is not what it looks or feels like in reality.

Do not underestimate your intuition and your gut feelings because in the moments of uncertainty, they can be the source of your salvation. Learn to listen to yourself, tune in with your inner voice and your inner wisdom that can often signal you a situation of danger. Be smart and respectful of your own thoughts and your own feelings, particularly women. I am sorry, but I am convinced that men and women are different, and that women are more sensitive.

And young girls must understand this because it can only help them manage interactions with boys better. Perhaps young people who grow up with siblings of the opposite sex have an advantage over people who don't have this opportunity because they are able to understand the characteristics of the opposite sex far better than someone who hasn't got a sibling of the other gender. What do they know about them then? How can they possibly figure out what they are about?

And nowadays I see more and more girls putting themselves out there on photos showing off their body, or literally pieces of their body, thinking that they have to highlight themselves for others. I'd like to ask them why. Pay attention to your body and to your spirit, and take good care of both. And to boys, I would suggest nurturing their kindness because I feel, often, that is what they lack towards young women, but it's, in my opinion, one of the most important virtues. I'm here to remind you of nurturing your kindness. Look girls in the eyes, see how that feels. Namaste!

Summary

- Adolescence
- Taking drugs
- Expecting older partners to protect you
- Being in charge of your safety
- Getting an education
- Sex in porn
- Boys, girls, and everybody else
- Selfies and bodies

Points for Reflection

1. Do you know any science facts related to the adolescent brain?

2. Do you think it's true that young people can be curious to try drugs?

3. What drugs do you know?

4. Do you know the effects of these drugs?

5. Can being high make you reckless?

6. Can you find an analogy between toddlers not perceiving dangers (like crossing the street), and high people not perceiving dangers (like having sex with someone whilst not being self-aware)?

7. Can people who are high be sure if they consent to sex, or different sexual acts?

8. Is it okay to have sex with someone who is high?

9. Can someone who is high on drugs be responsible for someone else's safety or feelings?

10. Who is responsible for your safety?

11. What are your resources for getting sexual and relationship education?

12. Do you know any useful books or websites? Please share.

13. Is sex portrayed in mainstream porn realistic? If yes, how? If not, what are the differences?

14. Do you believe that in general boys are unkind to girls?

15. Can thinking about all boys as not kind or sensitive towards other people be perceived as a gender stereotype and an insult to them?

16. Do you believe girls are in general more sensitive than boys?

17. Could identifying all girls as super sensitive and needing protection be perceived as stereotypical and very patronising to them?

18. What are the risks of accepting rigid gender stereotypes?

Points for Deeper Reflection

1. Feminist and Queer theory claim that for a long time, society has expected the genders to be and perform in prescribed gender stereotypes dictated by tradition and culture. Do you agree?

2. The full human experience is one where any gender can have any quality, regardless of stereotyped preconceptions, and embrace all the emotions that are part of being human. What do you think about that?

Your Notes and Critical Thoughts

Chapter 12
Wanting to Fit In

Sara, 42, Italy

*WARNING: Sexual Abuse Themes

What was the worst sexual experience of your adolescence?

The worst experience was my very first approach with a young man. I was 13 or 14 years of age, and I had just started to go to high school in a different city. So, I had started to travel to that city from home to meet new people. As school started, I became friends with some girls in my class. I was particularly interested in a group of girls who were the typical popular girls, who always moved in groups and who were particularly mindful of the way they looked.

They had been rather nice to me, so I decided to become their friend. They always used to dress very nicely, to apply make-up rather heavily and to wear high heels, and I also used to like doing those things because I felt I looked older. So, I started to emulate them and I also started to apply eyeliner to my eyes, and wear pearl earrings and nice shirts to go to school, which I had never done before.

Soon, I realised that this way of presenting myself was getting me the attention of the boys attending the last year of high school. I noticed the way they would stare at me as I walked across the corridors. On one hand, this used to make me feel happy, but on the other hand, I was nowhere near being ready to receive this kind of attention. I was just getting my head round the fact that this look was getting the attention of the boys, when I started to get the looks from a particular boy.

He was very handsome and I surely fancied him. Then one day after school, he approached me and invited me to go for a ride in his car, and as an idiot, I accepted. I was very embarrassed, but he kept complimenting me on how beautiful I was. Before I knew, I found myself very vulnerable. He unzipped his jeans, took out his penis and asked me to give him a blow job.

I was absolutely shocked. I told him to take me immediately back to school. I got very upset because I actually fancied him, whereas he went straight to the point as if he only saw me as a prostitute. This episode really traumatised me, and I started hating him, and I have hated him ever since. I'm telling you because this really impacted me in such a way…"

(She fights back the tears, her voice is unsteady, she apologises.)

Don't be sorry, you have nothing to apologise for.

I didn't speak about it to anyone.

(She struggles to speak and asks for a minute to recollect herself.)

I suddenly realised that I had not very much to do with those girls, and anyway, they weren't very interested in me and weren't particularly interesting themselves. Of course, they had nothing to do with what happened to me. I wasn't even hanging out with them outside school because I lived in a different city. However, the whole situation really felt like a huge explosion in my face. I realised that it wasn't right to expose myself in this way. This is what I thought. Luckily, I was able to make other friends in the class, girlfriends who were more similar to myself.

In terms of boys, from that moment on, I wasn't interested in them whatsoever. What made it such a bad experience was the fact that he had been so insensitive towards me. That boy cared for me just in the measure of the sexual performance I could have provided him.

Of course, I would've wanted something completely different from him. As much as I was attracted to him, I didn't want things to go that way, in a car, in a car park. And the way he spoke to me, I didn't like it at all. Who knows, maybe I could've ended up sleeping with him had he known how to behave himself, how to get to know me and if he had worked his way up to be in a relationship with me. But the way things happened, I ended up having a trauma which I have carried with me ever since. This was not how I had dreamt my first approach with a boy to be like.

Summary

- Wanting to look older
- Feeling attracted to other people
- Feeling entitled to receive sexual acts from others
- Treating girls as unpaid sex workers

Points for Reflection

1. Is it common for teenagers wanting to look older? Why?
2. Is it common for young people to find someone attractive?
3. Are there any parallels between the way the young man in this story expected Sara to perform a sexual service to him, and the way a client would ask a sex worker?
4. How would anyone being treated this way feel?
5. Is feeling entitled to receive sexual acts from others ever an acceptable behaviour?

What was the best sexual experience of your adolescence?

The best sexual experience as an adolescent was the one that followed the first time I had vaginal sex. That actual first time was something I remember like a funny anecdote, something between tragic and comic! However, it happened in quite a natural way, therefore it makes me smile rather than cry...; the best one was with a boy who was five years older than me, so I was 16 and he was 21.

He was a friend of my brother, and they were both studying at the University of Florence. He had come to ours with my brother for the Christmas holiday as a guest. That was an incredibly tender experience, which I hold dear to this day. He had Albanian origins, he was rather educated and well-spoken, and he had a foreign accent that I really liked. I fell in love with him pretty much immediately. Or maybe I wasn't in love with him, but I was definitely very attracted to him because he was a very charismatic person.

And I liked being around him. Once, we all went by car, I don't remember where to, but I remember it was a rather long trip. My parents were sitting in the front of the car, and my brother, he and I were sitting in the back of the car. It was evening, and quite dark. Suddenly, I felt his hand getting through my shirt, touching my chest. But he did it in such a gentle and soft way, it was the very first time that someone had touched my breasts in that way.

I thought how he was very cute and what he was doing was very enjoyable. Luckily, it was dark because it was late in the night by then. However, the whole thing was rather bonkers considering my parents were sitting in the front and my brother was sleeping next to us. It was so silent, and no one was looking at each other. And I didn't dare look at him because I guess I would've just burst out laughing. Another lovely thing he did was touch my lips ever so softly. That really made me melt. There definitely was a strong attraction between us.

The moment we got home, something like a hunting game started, and we were just trying to find the time and the place to be alone. In our house, there was a loft where there was a bed, so that's where we ended up finding each other. Nobody knew about us, neither my parents nor my brother—although at some point, my brother started to suspect something was actually happening between us. But I remember clearly thinking that I didn't even care if someone had found out because all I wanted was to be with him.

What I remember about us being together is, of course, the sex, which was very gentle and tender. But also the fact that after sex, he would fall asleep, and I would spend hours caressing him. For hours! He stayed with us the entire Christmas holiday period, and after that, both my brother and he went back to Florence. So, we started having a long-distance relationship. Of course, it was hard for me to go and visit him because I was only 16. I did what I could to see him where he was, but I knew that the relationship couldn't have carried on for much longer as an official relationship: he was attending university, and I was still in school.

At some point, he even asked me to choose between my parents and him, which obviously I couldn't do because I was too young to leave home. So, I can say that from this experience I have a beautiful memory. And I have continued to be in love with him ever since, really, precisely for the way he was—even though he wasn't a saint, as he was aware of his charisma and sex appeal, and I knew he was seeing other women. But I couldn't consider this equal to cheating because, after all, we were not officially boyfriend and girlfriend because of the geographical distance.

Summary

- Mutual attraction
- Tenderness and sex

Points for Reflection

1. How does it feel to be attracted to someone and to be reciprocated?

2. What are the benefits of being tender to your partner during sex?

Sara's Insights

I have always been a girl with low self-confidence. I didn't feel beautiful, at least not as attractive as the other gorgeous girls I knew. And I understand that lots of young people feel the same, so as soon as they receive attention from anyone, they tend to seize the opportunity because they think that it could be the opportunity of a lifetime. I would say to you to pay attention to this aspect and to understand you are worthy just the way you are. Don't go with the first person who pays you a couple of compliments, not even with the first one that you fancy. Be cautious, because as far as I'm concerned, the negative experience resulted from two factors: me not being cautious and getting in the car with someone I didn't know, and the lack of respect from that someone.

I understand that nowadays the dynamics are even more violent, at least as far as I know, and I understand that now sexual education is taught in schools. But I think that women in particular want to be treated well and gently; therefore, as soon as you get the faintest sign of someone not treating you the way you deserve to be treated, even though social media may tell you that low standards are acceptable, you must tune in with your individual parameters.

Therefore, what you must do is understand your parameters first of all, like for example what you like, what you would like to try and what you would never like a partner to do, and keep it in mind when you have a person in front of you. The moment someone walks all over these parameters, you walk away because that is definitely not the right path for you. You would be very likely to get a negative experience if you stayed, if you ignored your own standards. Unless you are someone who likes to take risks. In that case, go ahead and see what happens, but I can almost guarantee you that you will be left with a bitter taste in your mouth.

I also advise you to speak more to your friends, to find someone who can be close to you, who can listen to you and who can be there for you, so that if something happens to you or you are in doubt at least you can talk to them, because living a bad experience in solitude isn't nice. Don't feel ashamed and speak to someone you can trust and who can support you. Try to identify a person who could listen to you without judging you, such as a mother, an auntie or simply a friend. Anyone. We always know who such a person might be. This is it. These are all the insights I can offer given my experience. I don't have any more pearls of wisdom.

Summary

- Comparing yourself to others
- Settling for anything
- Being treated with respect and dignity
- Figuring out your parameters
- Sticking to what feels right

- Finding someone to confide in

Points for Reflection

1. People do it often, but why is it never constructive to compare ourselves to others?

2. Do you know anyone, young or old, who hasn't got any insecurities?

3. Is settling for anyone (for fear of missing out on an opportunity) likely to make you feel like you are really worthy?

4. Is it accurate to state that, however different we may be and whoever we may like, everyone wants to be treated with respect and dignity, no matter their gender?

5. How important is it to take time to figure out what (and who) you want?

6. How can people make sure they stick with what feels right?

7. If something unpleasant or even traumatic happened to you, who would you speak to? Why?

Your Notes and Critical Thoughts

Chapter 13
Don't Let Anyone Use You

Serena, 23, Italy

What was the worst sexual experience of your adolescence?

I was about 15 or 16 years of age, and she was my first girlfriend in high school. My body dysphoria has always been within me. However, it has matured in time. But this girl with whom I got together made me feel extremely guilty about being a woman. She almost made me feel ashamed of it. I have a beautiful memory on one hand, but an awful one in terms of our sex together.

I remember I didn't even have the courage to undress myself in front of her, and I would feel almost disgusted of feeling her hands on my body, on those parts of my body that are essentially female parts. There was always a wall between the two of us, and I remember clearly moments in which I would remove her hands from my body, and I would not get undressed. I would keep my clothes on my entire body.

Sometimes it got to the point where I would not even remove my shoes. Sex with her was about making her feel pleasure, and it was only about her. I was exclusively an accessory, the means to enable her to have pleasure, but I was completely foreign to the dynamic of actually feeling any pleasure myself. I can't tell you exactly why, I assumed that this was a consequence of not being able to trust the person that was in front of me. I liked being with her, but not to the depth of allowing her to literally touch with her hands who I really was, who I was externally, even though it wasn't who I felt internally. This inability to trust her with time led me to feel a real repulsion for her, and I am sorry to say that, because perhaps her behaviour was not on purpose, or she wasn't fully aware of its effects.

And because I was quite young, without trying to appear like super mature at the age of 23, I was rather inexperienced and I didn't know anything about the transgender world. These were my first attempts to approach this world, which up to that point had been completely unknown to me. I always had to research independently to find out about things that were affecting me, the different ways I was feeling and the reason behind my feelings in such ways.

There was always a gap between how this girl would say she would understand me and accept me, and the actual reality of our relationship. This resulted in me feeling like I had to protect myself to the extent of never allowing myself to open up to this person. So,

I have a very horrible memory of our relationship because, if I imagine ever being in her shoes, where someone removes my hands from their body, I wouldn't feel right. The way she used to touch my body made me feel guilty about being a woman.

She was only interested in my male side and not me in my entirety, in my contradictions, in me as a person, as a woman who was figuring out she actually felt like a man. The moment I would open up to her and talk about how I actually felt about my identity, she would say, "Okay, so from now on you're going to be a man." Of course, sometimes that made me feel happy; however, I wasn't ready for such a huge jump in such a forced way. I needed a gradual shift, I needed her to accept to be with me as a woman who wanted to be a man and who was working towards that, rather than to be treated as if I were a man already. I needed her to ask me what I needed.

So, I felt so ashamed of my body. So, here's a silly example: if I had to go to the toilet, I felt really embarrassed to pee in front of her because I would have had to sit down, so I would have had to be a woman. Before I knew it, we were living a total lie where I was forced to pretend to be already a man. I had to put myself in a man's shoes instead of naturally allowing myself to feel like a man in whichever measure, naturally. It was clear that she was in love and attracted only to that side of me and not to the entire person.

And even the rare times that we talked about it, she would say that she was there for me, but would also hint that she didn't know whether she would've been with me in the long term. She really made me feel so confused. What is more, she never challenged my removing her hands from my body, and it was never a case of us talking about this issue together and figuring out a solution or a way to move forward together. She never offered to do anything to make me feel better.

This was my very first experience with a girlfriend, so everything felt ecstatic and fantastic at the beginning, but with time, I had to come to terms with what our relationship actually entailed. Believe me, in my entire life, I never want to ever feel like a simple object used to provide pleasure. I also want to feel 100% involved in the dynamic of pleasure. That was the worst, feeling like an object and feeling unable to say "I am sorry, but today I don't feel like it" because, if I had said so, I felt that there would have been repercussions on our relationship.

I didn't know what else to do, so I decided to please her and limit myself to just watching her being pleased. I didn't feel like she actually understood me. Our relationship was just about who she needed me to be and never about what I wanted or what we could have wanted together. She was selfish; she was ckay with me giving her pleasure even though I wasn't feeling any pleasure in myself.

And then she ended up cheating on me with a man. That was the grand finale.

Summary

- Body dysphoria
- Being transgender
- Working things out in your own time
- Being with someone with body dysmorphia
- Using people
- Asymmetrical sex
- Asymmetrical relationships
- That feeling in the gut

Points for Reflection

1. What is body dysmorphia?
2. Who can have body dysmorphia?
3. What does 'being transgender' mean?
4. Can working out one's gender identity be confusing?
5. What would be the advantage of not rushing this process?
6. Who do you think would be good organizations in your city to support transgender people, or people affected by body dysmorphia?

7. Is it okay to use people just to get sexual pleasure off them?

8. In asymmetrical sex, one person has to provide the pleasure to the other, but the latter does not bother with reciprocating. Does that look like equality to you?

9. Is it likely that people involved in asymmetrical sex also have an asymmetrical relationship, where one person's needs in general are met, but not their partner's?

10. Have you ever had a feeling in your gut telling you that something isn't right for you? And did you follow it? (You don't have to tell what it was about!)

11. When you have an intuition about something, where in your body do you feel it? In your guts? In your heart? In your stomach? Where?

12. What are the advantages of trusting your gut feeling and following on with actions?

13. What may the risks of ignoring your gut feeling be?

Points for Deeper Reflection

1. How do you imagine you could support your partner if they had body dysmorphia?

2. Is it hard to trust your gut feeling and follow your inner wisdom? Please share your perspective.

What was the best sexual experience of your adolescence?

The most beautiful experience is the one I have been living for the last three years with my current girlfriend. Everything I have been talking about in the previous experience is the actual opposite of my current relationship. As much as the level of my dysphoria is quite high, thanks to the connection we have and the fact that she listens to me, she advises me and tries to put herself in my shoes, so when she touches my dysphoria with her hands, metaphorically speaking, and in the actual flesh, I feel fine. I don't feel dysphoric.

To think about it, it's a bit of a paradox; however, with her, I don't feel it that much. When she touches me, I feel I'm a man, even if she touches my breasts or my intimate parts. "It's crazy," I think to myself, "This can't be real!" But that's what happens with her because of the level of intimacy we have.

Our relationship feels to me like I am fine, and there's nothing I am going without. I have everything I want because, unlike everyone else I have been with before, she makes me feel like I am there 100%, I am present as I am. I always felt present 50% or 60%, or 70% in my previous relationships. Now, I am here completely. I am here with my female name, and I am here with my male name. I am here, regardless. It feels like I have reached a milestone which will be significant for the rest of my life.

I went from being ashamed to take my shirt off, to take my shirt off and, yes, still being ashamed of or uncomfortable with my breasts, but knowing that if she touches them, I feel fine, I feel safe. It absolutely feels like a personal victory, a victory that I honestly deserved after everything I have been through.

The most important factors in this relationship are our deep mutual understanding, the respect and the understanding of one another. Especially the deep mutual understanding, because that's fundamental in sex. If my partner doesn't tell me what she likes and what she doesn't like, and me her, if there isn't communication, there can't be a relationship. One can't take for granted that something sexual will be liked by their partner because different people like different things, clearly. So, having achieved a mutual trust that allows us to openly speak about these things without any sort of censorship, and making each other comfortable when sharing these things, makes me feel like I've got it all. When I know what she likes and she knows what I like, that's where there can be pleasure, desire and love. There is basically everything.

Summary

- Intimacy
- Self-acceptance
- Deserving to be accepted
- Communication
- Honouring your desires

Points for Reflection

1. What do you think of the level of intimacy described by Serena?

2. Is self-acceptance true self-love?

3. Is self-acceptance important even as you may be still in the process of figuring out aspects of yourself like gender identity or body dysmorphia?

4. Can you truly love another person if you don't love yourself?

5. How can you practice loving yourself?

6. Some people may think that if someone loves us, then they should be able to know (or guess) what we like and what we want. Do you think that is realistic?

7. Who is responsible for speaking up about what works for you and what doesn't?

8. What could be the benefits of asking for what you desire?

Serena's Insights

This might sound like rhetoric, but I think it's true: I would say to my younger self to wait for the right moment, and I would say that to all teenagers of the planet, too. Don't be in a hurry just because society is in a hurry for you to be sexually active or your friends are in a hurry to be sexually active. Don't give in to the pressure and to the idea that if you don't have sex by the age of 16, you're a loser. If you don't feel ready, then please wait because you may find yourself having a negative experience for which you're not equipped, which can deeply scar you and badly influence your future relationships, which would be a real shame. And all because you were in a rush to be able to run to your classmates and announce that the day before you had sex. Wait for the right moment, wait for love, wait to feel ready. I say these things precisely because when I was 15, I would have loved someone to come to me, put a hand on my shoulder and say, "Hey kid, you're not ready. Don't do it. Wait."

Summary

- Rushing being sexually active
- Expectations on teenagers
- Standing your ground

Points for Reflection

1. Do you think teenagers tend to be in a rush to become sexually active? If so, why?

2. Do you perceive any cultural and social pressure for teenagers to be sexually active?

3. What would be the benefits of standing your ground and waiting until you actually feel ready to be sexually active?

4. What do you think being sexually ready may feel like?

Your Notes and Critical Thoughts

Chapter 14
Being a Rape Survivor at a Young Age

Sandra, 20, Mexico

*WARNING: Rape and Sexual Abuse Themes

What has been the worst sexual experience of your adolescence?

My worst experience was when I was about 12 or 13 with a guy that I met in my music school, where I would study in the afternoon. I couldn't tell you that we were friends because he was 15 and in the year above my course, and we met literally in the hallway. He talked to me first and said hi, or whatever. Then he started to act friendly. I shouldn't say 'friendly' because the actual word should be 'weird'. Suddenly, he asked me to be his girlfriend, and I don't know why, but I said yes.

But at the same time, I didn't give it much importance. I didn't think it was much of a big deal. A week later, he invited me and my best friend to hang out at his place with him and his best friend, not to do anything in particular. We went there, and suddenly he asked me to go to his room to have a look at his new guitar. His family had lots of money, millions, so the notion that he might have a new guitar sounded perfectly plausible to me.

I followed him to his room, and my best friend stayed with his best friend. As soon as I entered the room, he pushed me onto the bed. He was a lot heavier than me. Now I am strong and tall, but at that time I was super skinny. I still remember very clearly how he very forcefully grabbed my hands and put them over my head to immobilise me. He was holding both of my hands with one single hand as he was very strong. He started touching me and ripping my clothes off; he managed to undo the bottom of my jeans and, basically, he raped me.

He started to have sex with me, but at some point, I managed to get my knee on the side and, somehow, I kicked him with my knee either on his tummy or his penis, I actually don't know. I mean, I kicked him pretty hard, so he got hurt, and I managed to push him away. I didn't knock him off, but he had turned to his side to protect himself, so I was able to get out of the room and join my friend.

I remember immediately texting my mum and asking her to come and pick me up. I was never able to tell my mum anything about what had happened for years. The experience was really horrible, particularly because I was still a child and that was my very first sexual encounter. Then my best friend told me that she had overheard him speaking to some friends of his about how he had won the bet: basically, he had bet with his friends that he was going to have sex with me, and that is why he had asked me to be his girlfriend out of the blue and he had invited me to his house.

I had never taken any notice of how weird he was being, but it all made sense later. I only told my mother a few years ago. So yeah, it took me a long while to talk to her. I had told some of my friends, and clearly my best friend, but not my mum. When she found out, she wanted to press charges against him, but I told her that it wouldn't have made any sense to do it after so many years because I wouldn't have had any proof. Also, his family is very rich. His father works in a bank or something. I think he came from a family where he was brought up thinking that he could get what he wanted as soon as he wanted it.

Summary

- Rape
- Not confiding in adults
- Reporting rape to the police

Points for Reflection

1. What is rape?

2. If you were a survivor of sexual violence, would you know who to ask for help?

3. What professional individuals support victims of sexual violence as part of their job?

4. In your city, is there adequate support in place for victims of sexual violence?

5. If you were a victim of sexual violence, would you consider using the Internet to search for the right support?

6. Can crime be fought adequately and systematically if it doesn't even get reported?

7. Whose choice ultimately is it reporting sexual violence?

8. May there be cultural barriers or particular personal circumstances that may influence a victim of sexual violence in the decision of reporting the crime or not?

9. How could you support a friend who does not feel safe in reporting this type of crime to the police?

10. Can fighting for justice be a positive process for a survivor of sexual violence, albeit a difficult one?

11. *Victim or survivor? Both perspectives are valid. The choice is personal. Some people identify as 'victims', a word that acknowledges the harm they've endured. Others reclaim*

'survivor' to reflect their strength and journey forward. There is no "right" label. There is no one path to healing. There are only personal stories and the individual right to name them. What do you think about this perspective?

How did your mum react when you told her?

I must say, it was a complete disaster. It was a complete disaster! I did tell her when I was about 18, but I never meant to. I told her in a bad way, during a fight. So, I have a heart condition, and she had taken me to a cardiologist because my old cardiologist had died.

Now, this new, horrible cardiologist decided that when he was sticking the electrolytes for the electrocardiogram on my chest, it was fine to touch my breasts, as if it was completely normal and part of the examination. At that moment, I completely froze and I didn't do anything, but when we got back to the car, I told my mum because I was still shaking. My mum reacted very badly, so I slammed the door of the car.

My mum didn't react appropriately because the secretary of this doctor was the sister of my mum's best friend. So, my mother didn't want me to tell anything because, otherwise, apparently, the secretary would end up losing her job. That was a horrible reaction from my mum, obviously.

Then a month later, I don't know why we were arguing, but I told her that she had reacted poorly, and how dare would she tell me not to say anything about what had happened at the cardiologist, when I had clearly been abused in front of her as she had been there, in the same room.

So, we were arguing, and I just snapped at her when she asked me why I hadn't told her there and then, in the cardiologist's room. I told her that, anyway, when I did tell her as we got in the car, she did nothing about it. Then it just came out of my mouth that that had been the second time it had happened to me, but that I couldn't tell her anything because she would react so poorly, so I would have ended up feeling even worse.

So, suddenly she asked me what I meant by it not being the first time, and I told her about having been raped… and she completely exploded. She said she felt incredibly guilty for not noticing anything and not having been there; she said how she had noticed that my personality around that time completely changed, that I was sad all the time, and I seemed to have many problems. She felt very guilty about not trying to understand the possible reasons behind my sudden change of behaviour.

So, she had a bit of a meltdown. I told her that I don't believe it was her fault. It is not her fault I was raped, and the fault is entirely of that guy. It's not even my fault; it's his fault. Anyway, she continues feeling very guilty to this day because she feels she put me in that situation.

And now I am doing an animation project at university about how women experience sexual violence, so she recently told me that she believes there are many things we need to talk about, but I told her that I don't need to talk about anything now because the project is not about me. But I know her, and what she's trying to say is that she feels very guilty and very sad about what happened to me.

Summary

- Sexual abuse
- Parents failing to protect their children
- Parents failing to prioritise their children
- Do not "rock the boat"
- Communication -or the lack of it
- Regrets

Points for Reflection

1. Sexual abuse can happen anywhere, from anyone and to anyone, and we must all be part of the solution. How do we do that?

2. If you were a parent, would you want to protect your child and report sexual violence to the police?

3. Is it acceptable for parents to prioritise the interests of others over reporting sexual abuse done to their children?

4. In your culture, is maintaining a certain image of the family prioritised over supporting the well-being of certain family members?

5. Do you believe that in your culture or in your family certain professions are excessively revered?

6. In your culture, is not drawing attention to the family for fear of embarrassment more important than doing right by some family members?

7. What are the advantages and disadvantages of telling a parent, your GP, or someone you trust in school about having been sexually abused?

8. Not reporting sexual abuse may seem like the easier thing to do in the short term, for whatever reason. But what may be the consequences in the long term in your opinion?

What was the best sexual experience of your adolescence?

I had my first consensual sexual experience when I was 15. It happened with my first serious boyfriend, and we had been together for a year to that point, more or less. I remember it was my 15th birthday celebration, so my family had rented a house just outside Mexico City to spend the weekend. My parents were there, and so were my best friends.

Clearly my parents' idea was to have the boys sleeping in one room and the girls sleeping in a different room, but that didn't happen! In the middle of the night, we swapped rooms, as I imagine many teenagers would be tempted to do! This rented house had many rooms, so my boyfriend and I sneaked to one of these bedrooms to be together. That was the first time I had an orgasm, so clearly that was for me the best experience!

(She laughs.)

Now, not many teenage girls get to have an orgasm during their first vaginal sex, usually because it takes time to understand what an orgasm is, and how to get there. And I remember I wasn't even very sure about what was happening to me or how an orgasm should feel. I didn't know whether that was what an orgasm would feel like, and obviously my boyfriend didn't know that either, so he asked me why it looked like sex was completely different, well, better for me. So, then we worked out that I had had an orgasm.

What made the experience great was that I remember I was generally feeling very, very happy about my birthday celebration. The whole weekend was pretty amazing, so I guess I was super excited and ecstatic in general, and I believe that that made me feel less restrained compared to previous sexual contacts, where I had felt slightly conscious. But, although that was a rented house, I had been there many times. So, the place was comfortable for me, and I think that had an impact on what happened.

I also felt very comfortable with that boyfriend because we had a very fun relationship. He cared for me, and I cared for him. I don't recall of any specific move he made during sex that made the orgasm happen. So, I believe it was probably the environment and the adrenaline of sneaking out of the room in secret. There were no particular moves there!

(She laughs loudly)

Summary

- When sex is fun
- Feeling at ease
- Bonding through fun
- Feminine Orgasm

Points for Reflection

1. Why do people have sex?
2. Is having sex in a comfortable environment important? Why?
3. Is feeling at ease with your partner fundamental to having a positive sexual experience?
4. Can you give some examples of how having fun with your friends can strengthen your bond? Does that work with relationships, too?
5. What other factors may contribute to sex feeling great?
6. What types of orgasm can people born with a clitoris have?

7. Did you know that there are around 4.000 nervous endings in a penis and around 8.000 in a clitoris?

8. Did you know that most of the components of the clitoris are under the skin and connective tissues of the vulva

9. And did you know that the overall size of a clitoris is around 9-11 cm?

Sandra's Insights

First, that sexuality is normal. It is something that we all experience sooner or later, and we are supposed to enjoy it. We have a lot of sexual education in our schools in Mexico from a young age, so we are very conscious about sex.

But I found that sex education was oriented to scare us, and it was more about "If you have sex, all these things can happen to you!" And it was not just about pregnancy, but about all the scary sexual transmitted diseases. Which is fair enough, but it is one single side of the whole story. And I don't believe that sex should feel scary. Sex is a magnificent thing that everyone can enjoy, so first of all, you are supposed to know that sex is there to have fun with and to enjoy!

Also, sex education should be about consent, which doesn't mean only saying 'yes' or 'no', but it is about things you like, or your partner likes, and it should be about how sex integrates other corporeal expressions as well, not just about vaginal penetration.

There are different types of sexuality that are perfectly natural and normal, and no one should judge a girl for having five or zero boyfriends in a month because it's perfectly fine. No one should find it okay to insult her or think that her value is less because of her relationships or sexuality. You have to respect everyone, because sexuality is nothing to be ashamed of, so you don't have to make fun of it. So, yes, probably I'd say that, I guess.

Summary

- Sexual Education based on fear.
- Different people, different sex
- Shaming girls for being sexually active

Points for Reflection

1. Has sexual education changed from the past? If so, how?

2. Some countries still teach sexual education focusing on fear and abstinence. Perchè?

3. We now understand that there are different sexual orientations. Do you know what they are?

4. There are many different ways to have sex as there are different sexualities. Do you also think they are natural and normal?

5. Shaming heterosexual girls or LGBTQI+ people for being sexually active but encouraging heterosexual boys to do the same thing is hypocritical and irrational. Can you explain why?

6. Do you think people who adopt double standards support gender equality and inclusivity?

7. Do you think that in your community there is still work to be done in educating people to treat everyone with the same dignity and respect?

Your Notes and Critical Thoughts

Chapter 15
Sexual Pleasure -
Who Is In Charge of Yours?

Judit, 44, Germany

What has been the best sexual experience of your adolescence?

Let's just say that I haven't had an experience that was particularly positive or particularly negative during adolescence. I guess my experiences could be divided into positive experiences and less positive experiences. The positive experiences happened where there were also deeper feelings involved. Personally, when I didn't feel there were mutual feelings of affection, I also felt a lack of intensity and meaning.

Amongst the positive experiences, I can mention my first penetrative experience and my first boyfriend. In both cases, I felt I was important to the other person and that they were interested in me as a person. This doesn't necessarily mean that these experiences were extraordinary. During my first time, nothing went particularly bad on any level, so I called that a success.

The relationship only lasted a month because it coincided with me spending the summer in a different town, having a summer job. After that, we both went home and lived far apart. Even though I had my first experience quite early, my next sexual experiences would be around three years later. I had sexual intercourse with a couple of guys with whom there wasn't any emotional connection. These experiences were actually not very good for my mental wellbeing.

With my first boyfriend, however, I felt like I would achieve something good when we were intimate because he clearly cared for me a lot. And that was palpable. That was a real relationship because we were friends as well, because we had mutual friends, and because of our mutual affection for each other. It was probably nothing over the top, but it was the first time I felt sex was a natural thing—like eating or sleeping—like a natural component of life.

Sex was certainly part of our daily life; however, only years later did I understand that it wasn't particularly satisfying for me. I never had an orgasm with him, but I didn't know that because, up to that point, I had never had an orgasm anyway, with someone or by myself. So, I had no idea about my orgasm capacity and I had no clue about what to try to achieve during sex. I thought that orgasm was the pleasure I was feeling during intercourse because, of course, it was pleasurable. But I never climaxed with him.

Summary

- Lack of basic sex education
- Not knowing one's body
- Sex and feelings

Points of Reflection

1. What do you think it might be like starting to have sexual experiences without basic sex education?
2. Could knowing how one's body works be useful before even starting to have sex with someone?
3. How could learning how to feel pleasure support people during sexual intercourse with others?
4. Is there culturally shame around masturbation?
5. If so, why do you think that is?
6. And if so, do you think it affects people of all genders in the same way? Why?
7. Would it matter to you that the person with whom you have sex deeply cares for you?

What was the worst sexual experience in your adolescence?

I have not had an experience that was particularly negative, but certainly they were mediocre because they felt like pure physical exercise, without any emotional connection whatsoever. And that happened with a particular guy who was quite into me. He actually really liked me. But his way of being intimate with me didn't feel special at all—it was horrible, actually! He clearly didn't have a clue about what to do to make his partner feel good during intercourse. Thinking of it, it was really horrible.

We didn't know each other very well, so there was no communication whatsoever between us. He had no idea how to please me, and I had no confidence to express myself and guide him. I didn't feel entitled to make any requests or share any needs. The sexual intercourse was pretty bad, so I certainly didn't want to go back there. I came to think that he didn't care about me as a person and that he was only interested in sex for himself, but perhaps he was probably clueless about how to be sexually intimate with someone. Perhaps no one up to that point had told him that whatever he was doing wasn't working. These encounters made me feel used. Or perhaps it's true that sexual chemistry is either there or not there.

In fact, as a young woman, the person with whom I had sex and with whom I had an orgasm was a complete idiot. Yet, he clearly knew what he was doing and we clearly had sexual chemistry. He obviously had done some research and was educated on how to be intimate with a woman, how to make her feel good and how to give her pleasure.

So, to begin with, I thought that this was probably destiny, and I had met someone able to make me feel incredible pleasure because of how deeply he cared for me. But this was an idea I had entirely manufactured in my head, and it had to clash with reality. He turned out to be dishonest and a so-called "player" with other girls as well. On one hand, he would write me poems and make me audio cassettes with music he had selected for me. On the other, not only did he have a girlfriend, but he was also having sex with other girls.

So, with time, I understood that his sexual performance wasn't inspired by feelings of love towards me; it was more like a badge of honour, something that made him feel gratified as a man. So, of course, having orgasms with him wasn't worth all the drama I had to go through. It was hard for me to make the decision to walk away, but I made a conscious decision to respect myself and my dignity.

Summary

- Sex and communication
- Responsibility for how you feel
- Feeling entitled to pleasure
- Sex and dishonesty

Points of Reflection

1. How important is communication during sex?

2. Do you think there still is an expectation particularly of heterosexual boys to be responsible for the outcome of a sexual encounter?

3. Can someone really be responsible for sexually pleasing someone when they don't know what that someone likes?

4. Is it okay that a responsibility that should be shared between two people may be put only on one of the two people?

5. Do you think that knowing how to ask for consent may have supported the young man in the first story in finding out about his partner's sexual preferences, or simply how she was feeling during sex?

6. Do you think that knowing how to express or withdraw consent would have helped Judit in sharing her preferences and express how she was feeling during sex?

7. Do you think all genders feel deserving of sexual pleasure in an equal way? Please share your point of view.

8. Has the term "player" a positive or a negative connotation?

9. Is it only referred to heterosexual men? If so, what is the counterpart for other genders and sexual orientations?

10. Why is being honest as important in a sexual hook-up as it is in a romantic relationship?

11. Can meaningful sexual consent even happen when someone misleads you on any level?

Judit's Insights

What I would've liked to know back then is that sexual pleasure does not necessarily go hand-in-hand with romantic feelings. There can be people with whom, because of sexual chemistry or because of their particular attitude and inclinations, there is an intense sexual compatibility. However, that doesn't mean that these people are going to be faithful, honest, and emotionally available to have a loving relationship.

I would've liked to know that it's possible to have a sexual relationship that is gratifying, but that doesn't necessarily mean that it will be accompanied by a great love story. And that's okay, if you consent to it.

I would've liked to know that feeling sexual pleasure is my right, it's fun, and it's natural. You don't necessarily have to be in a loving relationship to express and explore your sexuality, as long as there is mutual respect, clarity, and honesty. So sometimes, freeing yourself from the prejudice that you can only enjoy your sexuality if you are loved by your partner or in a romantic relationship can enable you to experience your sexuality and learn about yourself.

It is possible to have great sexual compatibility with someone and to have fun together even though you are not in love with each other. It is possible to have sex in a simple and lighter context, without being too serious.

I am not suggesting that I do not want a great sexual relationship within a deeply loving relationship—that is clearly the jackpot for me. But knowing that the two things can be separate has been liberating for me and has enabled me to recognise my sexual needs regardless of being in love or not.

I used to put a censorship on my desires and never dared to request anything because I thought it was something I couldn't do. I thought people offered what they could, and I didn't think it was polite to ask for anything. I know now the opposite is true.

I know now that it is not right to ask or expect someone to love you more, to have deeper feelings for you, but it is perfectly okay to ask someone to take better care of your body, and touch you and be physical with you in ways that you like.

Summary

- Romantic feelings and sexuality
- Getting to know yourself
- The basis for good sex

Points of Reflection

1. Is the idea that the best sex happens within a romantic relationship very common?

2. Can negative sexual experiences also occur within romantic relationships?

3. What may define great sex?

4. What are the basic conditions for any kind of relationship?

5. What does it take to have the confidence to ask your sexual partner for what you want?

Your Notes and Critical Thoughts

Chapter 16
Partner's Manipulation

Véronique, 22, France

*WARNING: Sexual Abuse Themes

What was the worst sexual experience in your adolescence?

It was with a boy I had met abroad when I was 18. I went to his house, and we spent some time together. He expected everything would go the way he wanted, ending with us having sexual intercourse. He had no manners whatsoever. I knew nothing about consent, and I was quite shy and not very confident as well.

As we started being physical, it soon became apparent that he had sexual preferences for sadism and masochism. He expected me to engage in some role play when I had already told him that I had not had many previous sexual experiences. He asked me to wear a collar attached to a leash, something you would expect to use when you go for a walk with your dog. I refused, but he kept on begging and begging, insisting and insisting.

When we started to have sex, I was very tense and didn't feel comfortable with him whatsoever—quite the opposite. I was tense and in a state of alert. I wasn't aroused at all, and because of that, the penetration wasn't happening.

So, instead of asking me what I would've liked to do with him, he proposed to have anal sex. I remember he kept asking and asking, making me feel like I was refusing to do something completely basic. He kept saying that his previous girlfriend did those sorts of things with him all the time, making me feel like there was something wrong with me for not jumping for joy at the idea of having sex with him that way.

He kept asking me to do things that, clearly, he had seen in pornographic movies—like oral sex in a very particular way, and finishing the act in a particular way. I was having none of it. I didn't fancy any of that. But he kept pestering me, so I ended up giving him oral sex the way he wanted it. I felt really humiliated afterwards. I felt really down. Somehow, I thought I owed it to him because I wasn't able to have vaginal penetrative sex. It's almost like I felt it was my duty to offer a viable alternative.

He had no respect for me, and you know what? He did absolutely nothing to please me, to give me pleasure. He didn't do any foreplay with me. He demanded I give him oral sex but told me clearly that he would not give me oral sex because that wasn't enjoyable to him; he would've gotten nothing out of it. It wasn't worth doing it for me.

I only realised afterwards that the reason why the penetration wasn't happening was because I wasn't sexually aroused, I wasn't relaxed. Quite the opposite! I was so tense and quietly freaking out inside. He just thought that it was enough to put some lubrication to allow the penetration in my body. But that doesn't work! If a woman isn't aroused, the penetration is not going to happen—unless you force yourself onto her.

The most devastating thing was the relentless insisting and the psychological manipulation that he kept trying on me to force me to comply. That was complete psychological manipulation. The whole thing was really traumatising and made me feel unable to trust anyone for a long time.

I had had another negative experience prior to this one, where I felt like pretty much the guy jumped on me without any foreplay and the penetration wasn't happening. I ended up feeling that there was something wrong with me, so I ended up going to a sexologist because I was worried about my anatomy and my inability to have penetrative sex.

The sexologist reassured me that there was nothing wrong with me or my anatomy, that I had a very distorted and negative idea of what sex is, and she took the time to explain the mechanics of penetration. She explained that it was perfectly normal that the penetration did not happen given the squalid circumstances and the arrogant sense of entitlement of the young man I had been intimate with.

But I think often, in similar circumstances, the blame goes to the girl. If she cannot be penetrated because she doesn't get wet or aroused, or if she doesn't climax, it is implied that there is something psychologically wrong with her. But the sexologist was very clear with me and said that the ones with the problems were my partners, not me.

Unfortunately, I really think nowadays many girls feel an obligation to sexually perform for boys, or even for their boyfriend, as if it were part of their job description as girls during hook-ups or in relationships. I think that we are conditioned by aggressive and sexist pornography and the social media narratives that revolve around female sexual performance. Possibly because, traditionally and culturally, in the past men were seen as entitled to impose themselves, to dominate women. This is completely unacceptable now that the concept of consent has been brought to the surface.

Summary
- Pornographic influence
- Psychological manipulation
- Inequality in sex
- Comparisons

- The basics of penetration
- Asking for help and guidance
- Sexual expectations
- Girls and sexual "duty"
- Consent

Points of Reflection

1. Is there nowadays a sexist, misogynist, pornographic influence on the sexual expectations of some heterosexual boys?

2. Is it realistic to expect girls enjoy enduring physical discomfort or pain, and psychological humiliation?

3. Can there be real consent when there is any form of manipulation or bullying between two people?

4. When someone is expected to perform a sexual act on a person, but this person has no intention to reciprocate, what does it mean? Do you think they are likely to be considered their equal?

5. Is comparison with the sexual behaviours of others a healthy and reliable criterion to make decisions on what you consent to in a sexual relationship?

6. Is there sufficient knowledge on the importance of foreplay to enable feminine bodies to get on the wavelength of pleasure?

7. As far as you know, can a person get sexually aroused when they are treated with arrogance, disrespect and contempt?

8. What could be the effects of feeling sexually used and abused on someone's self-confidence and overall mental health?

9. Do girls tend to feel inadequate or at fault when sexual relationships have negative results? If so, why is that in your opinion?

10. Or do boys have feelings of inadequacy as well? If so, what are they?

11. Do young people nowadays generally have a good network of support and guidance should they endure a similar experience?

12. What do you think of the idea that if a partner doesn't want to perform a certain sexual act, or it is not practical, then they owe it to their partner to please them in an alternative way even if they don't want to?

13. Do you think that a particular gender has more sexual expectations or entitlement than the others? Or do you think that all genders and sexual orientations may share this wrong entitlement in different ways?

14. *If you have to be convinced to do a sexual act, or talked into it, or bullied or shamed into doing it, that is not consent.* What do you think of this statement?

15. What does *enthusiastic consent* look like to you, and why is it important?

What was the best sexual experience in your adolescence?

The best sexual experience I have ever had is with my current boyfriend. He is the exact opposite of those boys. However, I met him when I was 20, so not during my adolescence. He's patient, kind, understanding, careful, respectful and loving. We talk so much, and our relationship doesn't revolve solely around sex. He is sweet and attentive to the feelings of the person in front of him.

So, we haven't rushed anything in sex and we gave ourselves plenty of time to explore sex together on our own terms. Little by little, we have achieved full vaginal penetration together. The communication between us is very good, and not only do I give pleasure to him but he also gives it to me. There is a sexual balance between us, and that has allowed me to become far more self-confident and to understand my body and the timing I need to feel pleasure. Not only have I realised that there is absolutely nothing wrong with me, but sex now is the best I've ever had.

Summary

- Awareness of your partner
- Self-awareness
- Communication

- Timing in exploring sex

Points of Reflection

1. How important is it to be aware of the person with whom you are being intimate?

2. Why is self-awareness important when you are being sexually intimate with someone?

3. Is being a good communicator beneficial to improving the quality of sex?

4. Who decides what the pace of exploring sexuality between two people is?

5. What may you and your partner miss out on if you rushed in being physical with each other?

Véronique's Insights

I think nowadays a lot of young people find themselves in this type of experience because they don't have enough self-confidence and trust in themselves. I would say that if someone is pushing you to do something you don't want to do and keeps insisting about it, don't do it just for the sake of it! There are plenty of nice people out there! There will be plenty of nice people in your life who will have a positive impact on you in the future, so don't settle with someone who forces you to do things you are not into.

If you don't want to do it, that's it—there's no room for negotiation. No means no! There is huge pressure from society, from porn, from social media to sexually perform. Be patient, someone nice will come along, and great sex will happen. You don't have to be somebody's sexual puppet. You can be a lot more than that.

Summary

• Pressure

• Self-pressure

• Cultural pressure

• Let others down, never yourself

Points of Reflection

1. How does pressure to perform sexually look like nowadays?

2. How does self-pressure look like?

3. How does cultural pressure look like?

4. Do you think some people may be less ready to let others down, but more ready to let themselves down? Why is that?

5. And what impacts may that have on somebody's life in the short and in the long term??

Your Notes and Critical Thoughts

Chapter 17
Personal Moral Values

Simone, 32, France

What was the best sexual experience in your adolescence?

I didn't have any sexual experience in my adolescence. I used to be a girl who would fall in love very intensely with someone, and I would hold on to the feeling—even for years. But these feelings were often not reciprocated. This really started before my adolescence, in primary school. I always operated in this way. In middle school or in high school, the person I was in love with could change, and that, again, would last for years. I would only manage to become their friend, and this was problematic for me. I thought there was something I didn't quite get, because I could see my peers getting involved with people or having first boyfriends and girlfriends.

In the later years of my adolescence, that became more of a problem because I decided I wanted to have some experience with someone, even if I were not in love with them. I began to think that it was enough for me to at least find them attractive. However, this became problematic for the boys, because the fact that I hadn't had any previous experience made them feel they had a bigger responsibility towards me. So nothing would happen.

At the time, I felt almost discriminated against, and the doubts in myself increased; I felt inadequate and sexually unlikable. Thinking about the whole situation through the years, I realised that this was actually a good way to filter out people who weren't really interested in me. What I mean is that if they had been in love with me, or even fancied me, the fact that I had not had any experience wouldn't have been an obstacle for them.

I always had it very clear in my head that I needed to fancy a person in order to become physically involved with them. I never gave up on this standard, because a person just being "good" was not enough. So the moment I realised that a guy had deep feelings for me but I didn't feel the same about him, I wouldn't take advantage of the situation just to gain some sort of experience. This was a principle for me. I wouldn't get involved with them just because they would've treated me very well.

Also, I don't think it would be right to get involved with someone knowing that they love us a lot more than we do, and vice versa. So, in the long term, I was okay with not having had any experience.

Even though I wasn't necessarily after *the man of my life*, I always knew that it was important for me to be emotionally involved with someone. I always knew I would like to get involved with someone whom I liked physically, mentally, and emotionally. I also think it is very important to have respect for the other person—whether I fancy them, love them, or whether they fancy or love me. I feel that if these elements are missing, the experience would be a let-down. It wouldn't be worth it; it would not be right for me or for them.

I think it is important to respect oneself and to respect the other person. This is fundamental, whether or not there might be some feelings of love.

Summary

- The dilemma of ' sexual experience'
- Contradicting feelings
- Personal values

Points of Reflection

1. Is there a specific point in time in which young people crave to experience intimacy with someone?
2. Does it happen to all people?

3. Is it possible to experience contradicting feelings between what we desire and our personal values?

4. How can the chance of becoming disappointment be minimised?

Simone's Insights

I believe respecting oneself and others is always the right thing to do, so I would advise anyone not to throw themselves into a situation just to be able to have sexual experience, because it wouldn't be that good—at least for one of the parties involved.

I believe it is wrong to get into a romantic or sexual relationship with someone knowing that they have feelings for us that we do not reciprocate, because it wouldn't be a fair and balanced relationship. It wouldn't be a healthy relationship.

I'm glad about how I behaved, because it would've been wrong to hurt people. To tell the truth, the situation was frustrating, but I always thought that it was more important to act according to my values and principles, and not just do something because my peers have done it and I haven't.

It's okay to wait to meet someone you like or love, and they like or love us: waiting is not a big deal because rushing things isn't worth it.

And I want to thank the people who didn't get involved with me because they realised I had deeper feelings. Even though back then it was tough for me because I felt frustrated and rejected, with time I've understood that they shared my exact same principles, and they also didn't want to hurt me or take advantage of me. They were adopting the same values that I would use myself.

It turns out that we actually had lots in common, and they were kind people. In time, I have appreciated their sensitivity and respect for me, which are absolutely wonderful qualities in human beings.

Summary

- Respect
- Unbalanced relationships
- Rushing vs being self-aware
- Not taking advantage of others

Points of Reflection

1. Why is respecting others important?
2. What may be the disadvantages of being in an unbalanced relationship?
3. Are there any advantages?
4. What principles do you think most young people have when it comes to having sexual rapports?
5. Is knowingly taking advantage of others in sexual and romantic relationships ever worth it?

Your Notes and Critical Thoughts

Chapter 18
Sexuality and Social Identity

Suryah, 52, England

What was the best sexual experience in your adolescence?

You know what? The best sexual experience was also the worst, which is quite interesting. It was not a full sexual experience; it was more about having a crush, and then finding out that they liked me too.

I was probably 14, and there was this boy at school that I liked. I was the only brown girl at school, so it was unusual for people to like me. I was more teased and ostracised than looked at as someone who was girlfriend material. So, he was taking quite a risk liking me, because he was a young white lad and we both lived in the same area.

He used to walk me home from school, and then, on about day five or six of him walking me home, he held my hand. It was so sweet and innocent, and I didn't really understand what that was about. It wasn't something we talked about at home, so whilst we did Sexual Health Education at school, that was about how babies were born. I didn't associate that subject with emotions and the feelings that come with having a relationship, because that was something that wasn't talked about. Not that it wasn't allowed—as an older teenager, I was allowed relationships.

So, it started with the handholding, and the crush, and the butterflies, and all of that eventually led to the first kiss, which was in a side street between some social housing in the area where I lived. And it was as if the whole world just got candy-coated in sugar. That's how it felt—to just have that connection.

I grew up in a very loving household, but it was a very practically run household: there were six children and my parents. It was very busy. So, there wasn't as much physical affection as there possibly could have been with so many children. And that moment felt like complete bliss—with that instant connection to another human being. So yes, that was my first and my best experience. It was very cute. It was new, it was the first time, and it was something I had only seen on TV.

Also, I had never felt connected to myself as a young woman. I didn't know what a period was, so when my period started, I thought there was something wrong with me. It wasn't a discussion that my mum or my dad had had with me and my sisters. And in a way, I was horrified. I thought, "Oh my God, I have to put up with this for the rest of my life! And the purpose of this is that I can have children, but it's such an inconvenience! And do people know it's an inconvenience?"

I had so many questions that nobody answered, and I think that made me feel insecure within myself as a young woman. As for having a physical relationship with somebody, I was thinking that those bits and pieces were just for childbearing, with no feelings that went alongside them. One, no one had spoken to me about them. Two, they were not acknowledged. And three, I wasn't aware that I could use them either.

So firstly—well—I wasn't white. I didn't have blonde hair and blue eyes. I didn't have the best clothes. My parents didn't have a lot of money, and I wasn't really allowed to go out at 14. My peers were all doing things and going out and having kisses, and that wasn't a world I thought I belonged to.

For me, everything connected—*except me as a woman*. Does that make sense?

So that was quite sad, really, which is why I absolutely made sure that when my daughter was growing up, I was having those conversations with her. I would've given anything for my mum to have had those conversations with me. And I didn't have any aunty who was close, so there was a void. I had an older sister, but that relationship was always quite fragile.

So, what was good about my first kiss is that it was about *me*, and it made me feel like I was part of that group, because I had now had my first kiss too. *I got it!*

And I was quite cute when I was young. And it wasn't that people didn't like me or didn't think I was cute or pretty, because I had a succession of boyfriends after that first one at school—four or five, actually. It was nice. It was interesting.

Some of the main aspects of those early experiences for me were about identity: the way I was viewed, labelled, or categorised as a young woman by others around me.

And actually, I do remember one particular girl who didn't like me very much, who made fun of that experience—and it became a tease—saying so-and-so kissed a *"Paki."* I am not Pakistani, but it just felt like race came into it. Was it about jealousy? Did that girl like that young man? Or maybe she could not understand why he liked *me* because she thought it was not allowed to like a brown girl.

There were so many factors, which probably wouldn't be relevant today because the world has changed so much—possibly. You know?

Another interesting dynamic is that we weren't a traditional family. I didn't know that I was Indian, and I really believed I was like everybody else. There were Asian boys and girls in school who would arrive in their traditional clothes and then change into a uniform—they would take the trousers off or the headscarf off. And I wasn't one of them. I was very different from them.

And yet, I was still put in that box of *'Other'*.

When you go through adolescence, you have a certain set of feelings—your first crush, you start tuning in to the fact of the gender you are—and this happens all over the world. That is part of growing up.

And yet, when you get put into a box, that experience gets tarnished with people's idea that you are different, and that you shouldn't be allowed to enjoy or experience that. That was quite harsh for my mental health as a young person.

To feel that there were natural opportunities and experiences for me that were somehow being frowned upon or controlled by other people's attitudes was a layer that affected my mental health as a young person—and particularly as a young person of colour. It really affected my confidence, and I was made to feel like I was not pretty too.

There was so much racism in 1976, when I started secondary school. And that is probably relevant today as well.

Summary

- The value of sex education
- Racial prejudice and discrimination
- The imposition of race-based sexual narratives

Points of Reflection

1. What do you think of current Relationship and Sex Education (RSE) in secondary schools?

2. Is RSE provided at home nowadays more than in the past?

3. Are young people satisfied with the RSE topics spoken about in school or at home?

4. Are there any RSE topics that are still overlooked or neglected in your opinion?

5. Is racial prejudice and discrimination still an issue today in the way young people socialise?

6. Are there still race-based social or sexual narratives imposed on the experience of young people nowadays?

*WARNING: Sexual Assault and Abuse Themes

What was the worst sexual experience in your adolescence?

My actual first sexual experience was the worst sexual experience, and I think that set the scene for continued feelings of low self-esteem and low confidence as a result.

So, I was probably around 15 and I was still at school. Every time I'd walk to school, I'd always see the same people. I started to recognise one person that would often try to talk to me, and eventually he talked to me. This would go on for months and months, until the pressure started for us to meet alone.

And I really had no guidance in those things, and I actually didn't know what sex was other than for making children. I didn't understand that it was an activity that two adults participated in to enjoy themselves. I also knew that it was a dirty thing. The idea in society, in my community, was that sex was something of shame because you should only do it when you were married and you only did it to have children. I think struggling with the shame attached to sex outside marriage is quite common for a lot of women around the world.

So, I was pursued by this person for weeks and weeks and weeks, and that ended up with me going to his house, which was probably the wrong thing to do, but I didn't know any better. And that ended up being my first sexual experience. The whole experience was more about what it meant to him – which was very little. He seemed to be in pursuit of having sex with someone who had not had sex before.

And I really didn't understand that. I remember afterwards making lots of phone calls to him, thinking that surely that was a relationship that would lead to marriage, because I didn't understand and I was confused. I was frightened leading up to it and even more frightened afterwards, because I felt vulnerable, exposed, and unclean, as if something precious had been taken away from me. I felt really dirty.

After that first experience, I felt dirty and a lot of shame. I did not really understand what had gone on. Then this other guy started to pursue me, I suppose because we would always walk the same way to go to school and back home. He started talking to me, and I felt quite vulnerable in that situation. But again, that ended up with me going to his house. He was older than me and I just didn't know what to expect. I thought that's what it was supposed to be: no romance, no emotional connection, almost like a control thing, like pulling you in under some control. It was very scary, and I didn't have anywhere to go for advice or support.

So, I ended up going to his house, and what happened was what I now understand as being raped, but I didn't understand then that that was what it was. Then he started to use that to blackmail me, to try and extort money from me – from my parents' business – and I gave it to him. I was really frightened: frightened about the repercussions, but also frightened about my family finding out about what had happened to me and that I was dirty.

What I didn't need after that situation, where I had been violated, abused, and taken advantage of, with no support and nobody to understand, was also having the whole school community looking down on me as if I were a piece of dirt. Now I was 16, but it felt like the same experience I had at the age of 14. Within those three years, I felt like my whole understanding of sex was that it was a control thing, used to make people feel bad, to control them, to use them, and to threaten them. It was really, really scary! I still feel that fear running through my body, and it is quite upsetting, actually.

But I remember I found the strength to talk to a teacher. I had a good teacher – he was a male teacher, my drama teacher. He was absolutely brilliant and supported me through that. Very soon after that, I left and went to college somewhere else to start doing my Art Foundation Studies, so I managed to get out of that area. But that stayed with me for years.

Obviously, I would know what to do now, but 40 years ago, in the early 80s, I had no idea. And really, if I had been more in touch with myself as a young woman, if I had been nurtured by my mother, possibly, things might have been different. She didn't really know what sex was herself, maybe. She got married at 16 and had three children by the time she was 20. Nobody was guiding me either, and information back then wasn't available. It wasn't something you'd talk about.

And that led me to years of feeling unworthy because of the rejection I felt when, after our sleeping together, he disappeared. That was awful. And I think that stayed with me for a very long time, certainly until my mid 20s, when I began to understand that, actually, I could control this. I've got some right about how this makes me feel. I can choose to participate or not; I can take advantage of the situation if that's what I want, if that satisfies the need that I have, or not. Eventually, I got to the point where I felt more empowered.

Summary

- Lacking sex education
- Being isolated
- Lacking self-confidence and maturity
- Sexual assault
- Being blackmail
- Asking for help

Points of Reflection

1. Are young people more educated around topics of RSE nowadays?

2. In your experience are there certain communities within which talking about sex is taboo?

3. Where can young people access the information they need, if they cannot ask at home?

4. Are young people mature enough to have sex at the age of 14 in your opinion?

5. What does the law say in this country?

6. Do you think the age selected by the law is appropriate?

7. Is it ever the victim's fault when someone rapes them?

8. Do you think there is enough support for victims of sexual violence?

9. Do you believe most young people are persuaded that talking to someone they trust is beneficial to get out of a risky situation?

10. Where can young people get help if they find themselves in a situation where they have been sexually assaulted and if they are being blackmailed?

11. Is this story similar to incidents of revenge porn? If so, how?

Suryah's Insights

There are a few things I'd like to share. Our body is our temple, and we own it. We have the right to do with it as we choose, and we also have the right to have it respected. It is vital to understand the difference between those two things: my rights and how I feel about myself, and what access to my body and myself I'm going to give to another person. For me, the fundamental principles of any relationship, whether it is physical or platonic, are trust, respect, and honesty. My person would have to have those three qualities, and they would find them in me. So please, cultivate relationships that give you that much. Also, if school is letting you down with the right education, and if at home certain topics are not discussed, go educate yourself. You are worthy of that much.

Summary
- Body sovereignty
- Self-awareness and consent
- Basic values
- Independent learning

Points of Reflection

1. What is body sovereignty to you?

2. What is the relationship between self-awareness and consent?

3. If one consents to a particular sexual act, does it mean that they consent to others?

4. Is it okay to change your mind on the consent given if your feelings or bodily sensations change during sex?

5. Can anyone, at any point during sex, retract their consent?

6. Sometimes it's difficult to know if you are going to enjoy a sexual act with someone, even if you have done it before. How could you manage a similar situation?

7. Do you also believe that trust, respect, and honesty are the basic, most important values to have with a partner, or can you add more?

8. What are the advantages and disadvantages of independent sex education learning nowadays?

9. Do you know any safe and reliable learning resources? Please share them.

Your Notes and Critical Thoughts

Chapter 19
Figuring Out Your Sexual Orientation

Beatrice, 22, Italy

*WARNING: Sexual Assault Themes

What was the worst sexual experience of your adolescence?

My first time was with a boy at the age of 14. I realised I liked girls when I was 15 years old, and after that I only went with girls until the age of 16, and that is when I understood that all the little problems I had had with boys were due to this reason. Therefore, I started to stay away from boys until after a couple of years I noticed this boy with whom I had a connection on an intellectual level.

We started to be in touch and to see each other; however, when we got to the point of sleeping together, the whole situation turned pretty tragic. First of all, I was no longer used to that kind of sex. I didn't feel at ease, and I was unable to even look him in the eyes or to touch him. I felt really uncomfortable, and because he was also as young and as inexperienced as I was, he was unable to put me at ease or to reassure me. Instead, he would tend to make me feel guilty for feeling uncomfortable by making comments such as, "Well, we all know that you're not really a lesbian, so what is your problem?" Now, because we lived in a small town, everyone knew that I had been with girls, so the mentality there isn't that people being bisexual are attracted by people, whichever sex they are. It was more the case of, "Now she's acting like a lesbian." I also had the impression that for this boy this was a little bit of a challenge – the ability to "re-convert" a girl to the penis. He probably would've felt like the king of the world had he succeeded, and I believe this was definitely a factor at play.

When we got to the actual point of having sex, there were several problems, including the mere problem of lubrication. So instead of doing anything about it, he would say that perhaps I wasn't in the mood to have sex, and therefore he would ask, "What are we doing then?" as though it was a waste of his time. He would really go for it, in terms of pulling a face and making me feel guilty about it. We tried it several times, but it never actually worked. On my behalf, I was mortified, as I felt like I had this huge problem and I didn't know what to do about it. He never really helped me, although he was the one that was supposed to put his penis into my vagina. I wasn't thinking straight because I was so embarrassed, due to somehow thinking that it was my fault and that I was the problem. In the end, it did happen in a horrible way, in a way that really *traumatised* me. What happened was that we had drunk quite a bit at a party, and then he followed me to the toilets. He decided that was the right place to penetrate me.

As far as I'm concerned, that really still feels like a kind of sexual abuse because of the way it happened: he just put it in, did his thing, and then left me there. If I think about it, it really was obscene. It became very clear that his intention all along had simply been penetrating me, putting his penis in my body and nothing more. It really was horrendous, so that has definitely been the worst experience I've had.

When I had first met him, I had felt this connection with him, and I was also wondering whether there was the possibility that I could also like boys. I was trying to figure things out and understand whether I should have not excluded boys altogether, so I wanted to explore, I wanted to understand. However, I chose the completely wrong person to do this. So, after the quick honeymoon at the beginning where everything seemed perfect, as soon as we started to have some challenges with sex, things started to go downhill pretty soon. It felt like he was a different person. He revealed himself as a selfish, superficial person. He revealed himself to be the stereotypical teenage boy who only thinks about *that* thing; those ones that, as much as they try to hide it and appear generally interested in you, in reality only want to achieve that one objective.

Of course, there are exceptions, but in truth it is necessary for girls to be careful and pay attention to this aspect.

The factors that have made it such a terrible experience have been my feeling wrong, first and foremost, my belief that I was the problem, the idea of not being able to be "normal", not being able to satisfy my partner, which were big factors. And yet, part of the enthusiasm I had in going out with him was the possibility to introduce him to my mother because, since then, my mum had not met any of my girlfriends. When I had told her that I liked girls, she had not taken it very well, and she was disappointed. Therefore, soon after I denied it and I made out like it wasn't anything serious, and that I actually liked boys, which wasn't true. I also had liked the idea of being able to walk around the streets without feeling frowned upon or being judged because I would have been in the company of a boy. All these factors influenced me in my decisions, and yet when it was about actually having sex with him, things never would turn out right.

On the physical level, I remember clearly how frustrated I used to feel, and of course, I was inexperienced, so I didn't manage the situation as I should have, specifically by telling him that in order for me to get wet he was supposed to engage in foreplay with me, for starters. Literally, I should have explained to him that just sticking his penis in my body doesn't actually work! So, I must admit that I was in the wrong as well for having been unable to take the situation in my own hands and take charge, one way or the other. And this was probably due to my insecurity, my inexperience, and my lack of self-esteem.

Summary·

- Figuring out your sexual orientation
- Coming out
- Societal pressure
- Sex and ego
- Putting pressure on your partner
- Lack of basic sex education

Points of Reflection

1. Figuring out your sexual orientation may take some time and experience. Is that okay?

2. How do you think it may feel coming out to your parent and feeling they are disappointed with you, or do not accept you for who you are?

3. How do you think it may feel when people try to convince you about who you are or who you should like and dismiss your choices?

4. Do you believe some people may see sexual relationships as sexual conquests or trophies to boost their self-importance or their ego?

5. What may that tell us about their self-confidence?

6. Is it okay to put pressure on a sexual partner to perform without paying any attention to how they are actually feeling?

7. What do you think about the fact that some young people may have no basic knowledge of how sex happens, and yet they still expect it to happen?

What was the best sexual experience of your adolescence?

I had the best experience with my ex-girlfriend, who is actually sitting in the other room!

(She giggles)

Not only has she been my longest relationship, but also in terms of affection I have never felt so comfortable and free as I felt with her in my entire life. I was 17 then. So, you can imagine how after that terrible experience I had had, I felt extremely uplifted when I met her. She really saved me because if it hadn't been for her, I would have fallen into a spiral of feeling wrong, feeling unworthy and all sorts of other negative things you're likely to think when you are an adolescent.

With her I felt truly happy, and in addition to feeling comfortable, it was a whole new thing in terms of pleasure. It was a completely different planet, and I really felt like I had found my place in the world. We ended up having a long relationship together, and we still are not fully capable of staying away from each other.

What made this experience so lovely was, first of all, our trust in each other and having an intimate connection. Also, I did not have the feeling of being under pressure or feeling like having to perform in such and such a way. Everything would feel just natural. I would feel completely at ease with her; therefore, the sex was driven by actual sexual desire and not by the idea of having to perform for the other person in a specific way, as it was expected by them.

Summary

- Feeling comfortable with a partner
- Mutual trust
- Desire-driven sex

Points of Reflection

1. What factors lead to feeling comfortable with a sexual partner?
2. What does it take for two people to trust each other?
3. Why do young people have sex, in your opinion?

Beatrice's Insights

First of all, understand that there are two of you in a relationship, so you shouldn't feel alone. Responsibility seldom resides in one single person, so there needs to be a balance. The most important thing is to try to understand each other, to meet in the middle, even if you are young. Just because you're not very experienced, that doesn't mean that the other person can decide for you. On the contrary, you must try to understand together, and together get to a decision on what to do. What I am trying to tell you is that if you don't feel ready, you shouldn't do anything just because your partner tells you to. What you choose to do together should be dictated by mutual desire.

For instance, I remember that even the first time I had penetrative sex, I went for it because all my friends were doing it already; therefore, I felt no other choice but to try it myself too. But the truth is that I hadn't felt the desire to do it at all. Honestly, I am talking specifically and more particularly to heterosexual girls. Don't put yourself in a situation where your boyfriend talks you *into* doing something, where he persuades you to do certain things in bed. Most teenage boys feel this unstoppable desire to have sex, any kind of sex, but I feel this isn't the same for most girls. What I am talking about is taking the time to understand your own body first of all, and to choose to share such experiences with someone with whom you have an intimate connection, a deep understanding of each other and a clear understanding of what each person wants.

If you feel that something isn't quite right, do not ignore it; rather, take your time to understand it, investigate where it comes from either with your partner or with someone else you can trust. In fact, if I could go back in time, I believe I would talk more to my mother about these issues because I believe she could have helped me to understand what was the right thing for me to do, considering how I was feeling. Also, and very importantly, listen to your own body.

There is something else I want to say. I am lucky; my mother isn't a bigot, and she's okay with sex before marriage, but I didn't know this when I was a teenager. I felt embarrassed talking to her about sex, even more so because of my specific sexual preferences, as she had not accepted it at the very beginning. But now we have such a good relationship, and we can talk about anything, including sex. I am able to ask her for advice, so had I known this when I was 16, I would have been able to talk to her and understand a lot of things that seemed so unclear back then. The ability of an adult you can trust to advise, to share their wisdom and to guide you is crucial because we often tend to speak about issues amongst ourselves, but the truth is that we are all inexperienced, and each experience can be different from the others.

For example, in my case, if my best friend had been heterosexual and had loved having sex with her boyfriend, that could have really influenced me in making me feel wrong because I was unable to conform to the "norm". Of course, if all parents were more open to this type of dialogue on multiple levels, including the non-heterosexual level, this would have a tremendous impact on young people. Or even if sex education at school was actually taught properly and it exceeded the idea of 'wearing a condom and that's that'; if sex education were more inclusive and open to talk about different sexual orientations, preferences and actual sexual desire instead of exclusively explaining reproduction, it would make a world of difference for teenagers. This is because teenagers start feeling different things about themselves rather suddenly, and it is so easy for them to feel wrong about who they are. So, if someone explained that there are many people just like them, it would be so much better, particularly because often home can feel like a hostile environment for Queer individuals.

Summary

- Building trust and companionship
- Building relationship skills
- Listening to your own body
- Heteronormativity
- Finding a trusted adult

- Peer pressure and life choices
- The importance of sex and relationship education

Points of Reflection

1. What are the advantages of learning to build trust and companionship in a relationship?
2. Is it possible to learn and build these skills even if you are young?
3. What does it mean to listen to your own body?
4. Do you think there is a societal expectation of people being "naturally" heterosexual?
5. Do you think homophobia is still very prominent in our society?
6. Do you think having a trusted adult with whom to talk about personal issues of gender identity or sexual orientation could make a real difference in a young person's life?
7. Do you have someone you can talk to?
8. Why is there so much peer pressure to have sex amongst young people in your opinion?
9. What are the potential disadvantages of making life choices based on peer pressure and expectations?
10. In your opinion, what could be the impact of RSE being LGBTQ+ inclusive on young people?

Your Notes and Critical Thoughts

Chapter 20
Cultural Shift

Sangita, 56, India

What was the best sexual experience of your adolescence?

There wasn't any in my adolescence. I don't think I had any good experience until I was in my mid-twenties and married the second time. I was born in England, but my parents came from India. I lived in a community where there were many Sikh families, so there wasn't any sexual experience to be had, because we weren't allowed. We went to school and we went to work. We weren't allowed to go out, like to clubs, we couldn't go to friends' houses… It just didn't happen in those days. I don't know about other families, but in my family, we just weren't.

In other Sikh families, boys were allowed to go out, but in my family, me and my sisters weren't allowed to go out. I mean, some of them were allowed to go with each other to school, and I don't know if anything sexual was going on secretly because in those days it was bad. You were not allowed to have a boyfriend. You weren't allowed to have anything physical. I certainly didn't. One of my Indian friends was seeing a boy, but I don't think anything physical happened.

Summary

- Different cultural perspectives
- Unequal autonomy

Points of Reflection

1. Are there different cultural approaches to young people being able to socialise in your community?
2. Do you know any culture in which there is a gender disparity in the autonomy and freedom granted to young people?
3. Do you know the historical background and civil consequences of such inequalities?
4. Do you believe these inequalities clash with modern democratic values of social equality?

*WARNING: Sexual Assault Themes

What was the worst sexual experience of your adolescence?

At the age of 17 or 18, I had an arranged marriage, and he had to come from India, and I had had no sexual encounters before then. I was told that he was three or four years older than me, but I don't know exactly how old he was. And in that family environment, when you got married, your mind and your body weren't your own. On my wedding day I was raped. And then these circumstances carried on for five years until he was deported.

Was he reported because you had gone to the police?

Yes. But it wasn't as simple as that. He was an illegal immigrant; he married me as an arranged marriage, and then we found out afterwards that he didn't have his papers. So, when we were called in by immigration, they asked us questions separately. And one of the interpreters looked at me and said, "You haven't agreed to any of this, have you?" And then there was a five-year battle because his family were relatively wealthy, they could pay solicitors and play around with all the legal loopholes with immigration and asylum seeking. And at the immigration office, they weren't bothered about the physical aspect of this; they were bothered about sending him back because that could have been seen as a marriage of convenience. But they didn't get me any support at all. I don't feel like I had enough support from my community; I feel like they just thought that's one of those things that just happen. I remember one of the older women said to me, "Men just can't control themselves when they get to that." And I think a lot of the older women and aunties had all experienced something similar. Imagine, back in those days, people would check your bed after the first time to see if there was blood or not. So it wasn't just the men who were promoting this behaviour, it was the women as well. It was the culture. It was very much the norm, and maybe they felt like I was making a big deal of it. And then, the police were no good, and they said they couldn't really do anything. But then again, we are talking about forty years ago. I didn't get any support from my family, or my sisters, you see, because the same thing happened to them as well.

Summary

- Systemic and traditional sexism
- Social enabling of rape
- Social expectations of a virgin bride
- Cultural patriarchy
- Systemic lack of institutional support

Points for Reflection

1. In your experience, are there any traditions that may support the enactment of sexism in your own culture?

2. In your experience, are there any social enablers of rape in your culture?

3. Do you think that in certain cultures there are still social expectations of a virgin bride?

4. Are there similar expectations for a virgin husband?

5. Do you think gender inequalities in families and communities may contribute to the rape of women being tolerated in society?

6. Do you believe that the police are a lot more focused on supporting victims of sexual violence nowadays compared to forty years ago?

7. Do you believe that families and communities are a lot more focused on supporting victims of sexual violence nowadays compared to forty years ago?

Sangita's Insights

Where I think it has changed a lot for me is with my daughter. We are open and talk about things. She's just gone off to university this year, and she's just entered her first relationship. And I wanted her first time to be a good experience and enable her to talk about things like this with me... You see, we were brought up very much in a way that sex was a hidden thing and quite a shameful thing to talk about, and actually the whole aspect of honour around a girl and her sexuality was that it is the honour of the family. But with my daughter, I think things have moved on rapidly. We have got a very open relationship. And my advice to her was that if you respect yourself, you will respect your body, and nobody owns it but you. And you don't have to do anything you don't want to do. And if you do want to do it, it's not shameful. And when she was entering her first physical relationship, she talked to me about it. So yes, I have experienced a huge shift during my lifetime, in my family, in my community.

With my oldest son, I also told him about my experience. When I told him about my forced marriage, he was perhaps a little bit too young. He just cried. He was sixteen. He also talks to me about his relationships and when he sees someone. I have really instilled in him that whatever he does has to do with care and love because it could scar somebody for life.

And if someone changes their mind, it doesn't matter at what stage they change their mind, they have a right to, just as he does as well. Because boys are also vulnerable. They're lost. Things have changed a lot in what they see in the media, and what they think girls want. But girls, even the ones that are more confident, ultimately want to feel cared about. And so that is what I have said to my youngest son too.

Summary

- Sex and shame

- Sexual experience and family honour

- Body ownership

- Family's support

- Consent and boys

- Gender representations in media

- Wanting to feel cared about

Points for Reflection

1. Do you think in your own culture there is an idea that sex is shameful when it is not done within a marriage?

2. Do you believe that in certain cultures sexual experience is attached to an idea of 'honour'? If so, can you define what 'honour' means? And how does it relate to a human being experiencing sex?

3. Is this idea attached to one gender in particular? And if so, how does that align with principles of gender equality?

4. How does it feel to know your body belongs to you and nobody else?

5. Do you think some young people may struggle with putting this fundamental principle into practice in their lived experience?

6. Do you believe that parents are increasingly becoming aware of the importance of their contribution to educating their children on issues around sex?

7. Do you believe boys feel confident in their right to deny or withdraw consent? If not, why do you think is that? And if not, how does that align with the principle of gender equality?

8. Do you think certain gender stereotypes may interfere with a young man feeling confident in refusing to have sex?

9. Do you think certain representations of gender in the media may be confusing? If so, how?

10. Do you believe it is true that boys are confused about what girls want? If so, why?

11. In your experience, do young people often try to adhere to gender-stereotyped behaviours they see in media, even in sexual or romantic relationships?

12. Do young people want to feel cared about in sexual and romantic relationships regardless of their gender and sexual orientation, or are there differences?

Further Insights from Sangita

I would say to young people: don't think that all boys are the same and all men are the same. For instance, me and my four sisters, we all had arranged marriages. But on the first wedding night, the husband of one of my sisters drew an invisible line on the bed between the two of them and said that he wouldn't cross the line until she was ready. And some of my friends have had a similar experience too. So, you see, not all boys are the same. I think that difference between young men has a lot to do with their family and how they were brought up, and their personality.

If boys are brought up to think that they can dominate when it comes to having sex, then that is the way they will act. The mind needs to shift. We do not think that boys are just like that, they cannot control themselves and they are animalistic because that would mean belittling them and taking away their intelligence. That is counter-productive for everybody. You would almost disempower your own boys by saying that they cannot control their energy, that they are helpless.

Whereas they need to be educated that they are in control. But quite simply, you don't always get what you want. And that goes for all genders. But you see, it starts at home. If there isn't equality at home between the parents, then, subconsciously, you have those same models outside. So if in the household, the mother or the grandmother are still submissive to their husbands, then those kinds of patterns continue through life.

At school, boys really need to be taught and challenged to put themselves into a woman's shoes, because that's when it's going to change. You will find, in my experience, some of the most gentle boys are the ones who've been surrounded by women. The shift needs to happen on so many levels.

Summary

- Boys, men, and generalisation
- Gender stereotyping vs reality
- Boys: nature and nurture
- Sexism and misogyny in the family
- Putting boys in a box
- Lack of gender equality in the home
- The role of school
- Learning empathy
- The shift of mutual understanding

Points for Reflection

1. In your experience, is there a cultural tendency of thinking that all boys are the same, and all men are the same?

2. Why do you think this may happen?

3. In your experience, can people of a particular gender all be the same?

4. How may a negative generalisation of boys and men affect the way they feel about themselves?

5. How may a negative generalisation of boys and men affect the way they behave with other boys and girls?

6. Do you agree that the way a young man behaves is individual and depends on their personality and the way their family brought him up?

7. What do you think impacts more on the way a young man behaves: their personality or the way they are brought up?

8. Do you agree that if a young man is brought up in a family where there are sexism and misogyny, then that will be mirrored in the way they behave with girls and in a sexually violent behaviour? Or may his behaviour be different?

9. How can a lack of equality between the parents influence the behaviour of young men? And young women?

10. Do you believe nowadays boys are thought to be violent and unable to control themselves when it comes to sex?

11. Have you ever come across someone who has this negative prejudice towards boys in general?

12. Do you believe that this kind of prejudice may be belittling, unfair and also insulting towards young men?

13. How important is it for the school to ensure young people learn about gender equality?

14. Is it important to learn to put yourself in the shoes of people of a different gender from time to time?

15. How may that impact your understanding of them?

16. How may that impact how you behave with them?

17. Do you feel optimistic that a profound shift in the understanding between different genders is taking place? If not, why? If yes, could you give some examples?

18. Think about your family, your community, your friends, and your school: what could you do in your everyday life to contribute to this fundamental shift to continue?

Your Notes and Critical Thoughts

Legal Aspects of Consent Issued by the British Government

Consent occurs when one person voluntarily agrees to the proposal or desires of another. In sexual relations, someone consents to vaginal, anal or oral penetration only if *s/he* agrees by choice to that penetration and has the freedom and capacity to make that choice. Consent to sexual activity may be given to one sort of sexual activity but not another, e.g. to vaginal but not anal sex, or penetration with conditions, such as wearing a condom. Consent can be withdrawn at any time during sexual activity and each time activity occurs.

Capacity to Consent

Issues to consider include whether the complainant had the capacity to consent if:

- *s/he was under the influence of drink or drugs;*
- *s/he suffers from a medical condition which limits their ability to consent or communicate consent;*
- *s/he has a mental health problem or learning disabilities;*
- *s/he was asleep or unconscious.*

Freedom to Consent

- Issues to consider include whether the complainant had the freedom to consent, for example, in situations such as:

- *Domestic violence – where a partner or family member may use force or power to remove a complainant's freedom to consent;*

- *Where the suspect was in a position of power where they could abuse their trust, especially because of their position or status – e.g. a family member, teacher, religious leader, employer, gang member, carer, doctor;*

- *The complainant was dependent on the suspect, e.g. financially or for care;*

- *If the complainant was young, was s/he significantly younger?*

- *Was the complainant old enough to consent?*

Steps Taken to Obtain Consent

- *Enquiring as to how the suspect knew or believed the complainant was consenting to sex, and that s/he continued to consent;*

- *Investigating whether the suspect targeted or exploited the victim at a time when s/he was most vulnerable.*

Reasonable Belief in Consent

- *Recognising or ignoring any signs from the complainant that they did not want sexual activity;*

- *Checking if consent was given for all the sex acts and not just some, e.g. consent for sexual intercourse but not oral sex.*

Addressing Myths and Stereotypes

- *The form of dress a person wears does not mean they should expect to be raped.*

- *The majority of rape cases involve an offender and complainant who know each other.*

- *Trauma can affect memory and create inconsistency.*

- *Being drunk makes the complainant vulnerable. It does not mean they were 'asking for it'.*

- *Most victims do not fight; resistance and self-protection/defence can be through dissociation, freezing, or trying to befriend the defendant – in fact, any effort to prevent, stop or limit the event. It does not have to succeed to be considered an 'effort'.*

- *Late reporting may be due to an inability to cope with the trauma of the incident, fear of repercussions, recognition of the abuse with maturity, control by the complainant, or fear of going to court.*

Glossary

Abortion: The deliberate termination of a pregnancy, most often performed during the first 28 weeks of pregnancy. Common reasons for inducing an abortion are birth-timing and limiting family size. Other reasons include maternal health, an inability to afford a child, domestic violence, lack of support, feelings of being too young, wishing to complete an education or advance a career, and not being able, or willing, to raise a child conceived as a result of rape or incest. When done legally in industrialized societies, induced abortion is one of the safest procedures in medicine. Modern methods use medication or surgery for abortions.

Agency: the ability to take action or to choose what action to take; the capacity of individuals to have the power and resources to fulfil their potential. Agency may either be classified as unconscious, involuntary behaviour, or purposeful, goal directed activity (intentional action). An agent typically has some sort of immediate awareness of their physical activity and the goals that the activity is aimed at realizing. In 'goal directed action' an agent implements

Awareness: It may refer to an internal state, such as a visceral feeling, or on external events by way of sensory perception. It is analogous to sensing something, a process distinguished from observing and perceiving. Awareness is also associated with consciousness in the sense that it denotes a fundamental experience such as a feeling or intuition that accompanies the experience of phenomena. Specifically, this is referred to as awareness of experience.

Bullying: Bullying is the use of force, coercion, hurtful teasing, comments, or threats, in order to abuse, aggressively dominate, or intimidate one or more others. The behavior is often repeated and habitual. One essential prerequisite is the perception (by the bully or by others) that an imbalance of physical or social power exists or is currently present. This perceived presence of physical or social imbalance is what distinguishes the behavior of bullyism from an conflict in a specific time and space. Bullying can be performed individually or by a group, typically referred to as mobbing, in which the bully may have one or more followers who are willing to assist the primary bully or who reinforce the bully's behavior by providing positive feedback such as laughing. Bullying in school and in the workplace is also referred to as "peer abuse. Individual bullying is usually characterized by a person using coercive, intimidating, or hurtful words or comments, exerting threatening or intimidating behavior, or using harmful physical force in order to gain power over another person.

Dignity: is the right of a person to be valued and respected for their own sake, and to be treated ethically. In this context, it is of significance in morality, ethics, law and politics as an extension of the Enlightenment-era concepts of inherent, inalienable rights. The content of contemporary dignity is derived from the Universal Declaration of Human Rights of 1948, summarized in the principle that every human being has the right to human dignity. In Article 1, it is stipulated that 'All human beings are born free and equal in dignity and rights. They are endowed with reason and conscience and should act towards one another in a spirit of brotherhood.

Dysmorphia: more specifically, Body Dysmorphic Disorder (BDD), is a mental health condition where individuals are preoccupied with a perceived flaw in their appearance, even though the perceived flaw is minor or not noticeable to others. This preoccupation leads to significant distress and can interfere with daily life.

Empowerment: the degree of autonomy and self-determination in people and in communities. This enables them to represent their interests in a responsible and self-determined way, acting on their own authority. It is the process of becoming stronger and more confident, especially in controlling one's life and claiming one's rights. Empowerment as action refers both to the process of self-empowerment and to professional support of people, which enables them to overcome their sense of powerlessness and lack of influence, and to recognize and use their resources.

Entitlement Mentality: in psychology it is defined as a sense of deservingness or being owed a favor when little or nothing has been done to deserve special treatment; the belief that one is inherently deserving of privileges or special treatment (the phrase "sense of entitlement" is often used). Entitlement can be seen through the actions of the individual, such as having a belief that they deserve the rewards which are due to their position, despite not performing effectively.

Female Genital Mutilation: the practice, traditional in some cultures, of partially or totally removing the external genitalia of girls and young women for non-medical reasons. It is illegal in many countries, including the UK.

Feminism: it is a range of socio-political movements and ideologies that aim to define and establish the political, economic, personal, and social equality of the sexes. Feminism holds the position that modern societies are patriarchal—they prioritize the male point of view—and that women are treated unjustly in these societies. Efforts to change this include fighting against gender stereotypes and improving educational, professional, and interpersonal opportunities and outcomes for women. Originating in late 18th-century Europe, feminist movements have campaigned and continue to campaign for women's rights, including the right to vote, run for public office, work, earn equal pay, own property, receive education, enter into contracts, have equal rights within marriage, and maternity leave. Feminists have also worked to ensure access to contraception, legal abortions, and social integration; and to protect women and girls from sexual assault, sexual harassment, and domestic violence. Changes in female dress standards and acceptable physical activities for women have also been part of feminist movements.

Many scholars consider feminist campaigns to be a main force behind major historical societal changes for women's rights, particularly in the West, where they are near-universally credited with achieving women's suffrage, gender-neutral language, reproductive rights for women (including access to contraceptives and abortion), and the right to enter into contracts and own property. Although feminist advocacy is, and has been, mainly focused on women's rights, some argue for the inclusion of men's liberation within its aims, because they believe that men are also harmed by traditional gender roles.

Feminism (Intersectional): it is a framework that examines how various social and political identities (like race, class, gender, and sexual orientation) combine to create unique experiences of discrimination and privilege. It recognizes that these intersecting identities can result in forms of oppression that are distinct from the experiences of people who experience only one form of discrimination.

Feminist Theory: it emerged from feminist movements and aims to understand the nature of gender inequality by examining women's social roles and lived experiences. Feminist theorists have developed theories in a variety of disciplines in order to respond to issues concerning gender.

Fight, Flight or Freeze: describe the three primary physiological responses the body has to perceived threats or stress. These responses are automatic, instinctive reactions aimed at self-preservation. The **"fight"** response involves confronting the threat aggressively, the **"flight"** response involves escaping the threat, and the **"freeze"** response involves becoming immobile, unresponsive or paralised. This response is often accompanied by a sense of being unable to move or react to the perceived threat. This can be a way of avoiding further harm.

Foreplay: a set of emotionally and physically intimate acts between one or more people meant to create sexual arousal and desire for sexual activity. Although foreplay is typically understood as physical sexual activity, nonphysical activities, such as mental or verbal acts, may in some contexts be foreplay. It can consist of various sexual practices such as kissing, sexual touching, removing clothes, oral sex, manual sex, sexual games, and more. Foreplay is not only about initiating sexual activity but is fundamentally centered on enhancing pleasure for all participants. It serves as a critical phase in sexual encounters that heightens emotional intimacy and physical pleasure, making the sexual experience more fulfilling and satisfying.

Gender Stereotype: a widely held belief about the characteristics, behaviours, and roles associated with a particular gender, often based on generalisations and assumptions. These stereotypes can be positive or negative, but they all limit individuals by suggesting that certain traits and behaviours are uniquely or exclusively associated with one gender.

Intuition: is the ability to acquire knowledge without recourse to conscious reasoning or needing an explanation. Different fields use the word "intuition" in very different ways, including but not limited to: direct access to unconscious knowledge; unconscious cognition; gut feelings; inner sensing; inner insight to unconscious pattern-recognition; and the ability to understand something instinctively, without any need for conscious reasoning.

Manipulation: in psychology it is defined as an action designed to influence or control another person, usually in an underhanded or subtle manner which facilitates one's personal aims. Methods someone may use to manipulate another person may include seduction, suggestion, coercion, and blackmail. Manipulation is generally considered a dishonest form of social influence as it is used at the expense of others. Humans are inherently capable of manipulative and deceptive behaviour, with the main differences being that of specific personality characteristics or disorders.

Masturbation: is a form of autoeroticism in which a person sexually stimulates their own genitals for sexual arousal or other sexual pleasure, usually to the point of orgasm. Stimulation may involve the use of hands, everyday objects or sex toys. Masturbation may also be performed with a sex partner and this is known as "mutual masturbation". Masturbation is frequent in both sexes. Various medical and psychological benefits have been attributed to a healthy attitude toward sexual activity in general and to masturbation in particular. Masturbation is considered by clinicians to be a healthy, normal part of sexual enjoyment.

Misogyny: the hatred of, contempt for, or prejudice against women or girls. It is a form of sexism that can keep women at a lower social status than men, thus maintaining the social roles of patriarchy. Misogyny has been widely practised for thousands of years. It is reflected in art, literature, human societal structure, historical events, mythology, philosophy, and religion worldwide. An example of misogyny is violence against women, which includes domestic violence and, in its most extreme forms, misogynist terrorism and femicide. Misogyny also often operates through sexual harassment, coercion, and psychological techniques aimed at controlling women, and by legally or socially excluding women from full citizenship. In some cases, misogyny rewards women for accepting an inferior status. Misogyny can be understood both as an attitude held by individuals, primarily by men, and as a widespread cultural custom or system. Sometimes misogyny manifests in obvious and bold ways; other times it is more subtle or disguised in ways that provide plausible deniability. In feminist thought, misogyny also includes the rejection of feminine qualities. It holds in contempt institutions, work, hobbies, or habits associated with women, and it rejects any aspects of men that are seen as feminine or unmanly. Racism and other prejudices may reinforce and overlap with misogyny.

Orgasm: (from Greek orgasmos; "excitement, swelling"), sexual climax, or simply climax, is the sudden release of accumulated sexual excitement during the sexual response cycle, characterized by intense sexual pleasure resulting in rhythmic, involuntary muscular contractions in the pelvic region. Orgasms are controlled by the involuntary or autonomic nervous system and are experienced by both males and females; the body's response includes muscular spasms (in multiple areas), a general euphoric sensation, and, frequently, body movements and vocalizations. The period after orgasm (known as the resolution phase) is typically a relaxing experience after the release of the neurohormones oxytocin and prolactin, as well as endorphins (or "endogenous morphine").

Patriarchy: is a social system in which positions of authority are primarily held by men. The term patriarchy is used both in anthropology to describe a family or clan controlled by the father or eldest male or group of males, and in feminist theory to describe a broader social structure in which men as a group dominate society. Patriarchal socialization processes are primarily responsible for establishing gender roles and gender inequity as instruments of power and have become social norms to maintain control over women. Historically, patriarchy has manifested itself in the social, legal, political, religious, and economic organization of a range of different cultures. Most contemporary societies are, in practice, patriarchal.

Peer-Pressure: a direct or indirect influence on peers, i.e., members of social groups with similar interests and experiences, or social statuses. Members of a peer group are more likely to influence a person's beliefs, values, religion and behavior. A group or individual may be encouraged and want to follow their peers by changing their attitudes, values or behaviors to conform to those of the influencing group or individual. For the individual affected by peer pressure, this can have both a positive or negative effect on them. Peer pressure can affect individuals of all ethnic groups, genders and ages. Researchers have frequently studied the effects of peer pressure on children and on adolescents, and in popular discourse the term "peer pressure" is used most often with reference to those age-groups. It's important to understand that for children of adolescent age, they are faced with finding their identity, which can be confusing. In other words, children are trying to find a sense of belonging and are the most susceptible to peer pressure as a form of acceptance. For children, the themes most commonly studied are their abilities for independent decision-making. For adolescents, peer pressure's relationships to sexual intercourse and substance abuse have been significantly researched. Peer pressure can be experienced through both face-to-face interaction and through digital interaction. Social media offers opportunities for adolescents and adults alike to instill and/or experience pressure every day.

Queer Theory: is a field of study that challenges traditional understandings of gender and sexuality, questioning the idea of fixed identities and norms. It explores how societal norms around sexuality and gender are constructed and maintained, often through language and power structures. Originating in the late 20th century, it emerged from lesbian, gay, and gender studies and is informed by thinkers like Judith Butler and Michel Foucault.

Rape: a type of sexual assault involving sexual intercourse, or other forms of sexual penetration, carried out against a person without consent. The act may be carried out by physical force, coercion, abuse of authority, or against a person who is incapable of giving valid consent, such as one who is unconscious, incapacitated, has an intellectual disability, or is below the legal age of consent (statutory rape). The term rape is sometimes casually used interchangeably with the term sexual assault.

Rape Culture: a setting, as described by some sociological theories, in which rape is pervasive and normalized due to that setting's attitudes about gender and sexuality. Behaviours commonly associated with rape culture include victim blaming, slut-shaming, sexual objectification, trivialization of rape, denial of widespread rape, refusal to acknowledge the harm caused by sexual violence, or some combination of these

Respect: also called esteem, is a positive feeling or deferential action shown towards someone or something considered important or held in high esteem or regard. It conveys a sense of admiration for good or valuable qualities. It is also the process of honouring someone by exhibiting care, concern, or consideration for their needs or feelings.

Responsibility: moral responsibility is the status of morally deserving praise, blame, reward, or punishment for an act or omission in accordance with one's moral obligations. Deciding what (if anything) counts as "morally obligatory" is a principal concern of ethics. Philosophers refer to people who have moral responsibility for an action as "moral agents". Agents have the capability to reflect upon their situation, to form intentions about how they will act, and then to carry out that action. In moral philosophy, a moral agent is an individual capable of distinguishing between good and evil and acting accordingly, taking responsibility for his own actions. This implies the ability to reflect on one's actions, evaluate the consequences and choose between different alternatives, taking into account ethical principles. In other words, a moral agent is not only able to act, but also to morally judge his own actions and those of others, taking responsibility for the consequences of such actions. Moral responsibility does not necessarily equate to legal responsibility. A person is legally responsible for an event when a legal system is liable to penalise that person for that event. Although it may often be the case that when a person is morally responsible for an act, they are also legally responsible for it, the two states do not always coincide.

Self-Awareness: the ability to tune in to your feelings, thoughts, and actions. In philosophy, self-awareness is the awareness and reflection of one's own personality or individuality, including traits, feelings, and behaviours. While consciousness is being aware of one's body and environment, self-awareness is the recognition of that consciousness. Self-awareness is how an individual experiences and understands their own character, feelings, motives, and desires. Being self-aware also means being able to recognise how other people see you. People who are self-aware recognise their strengths and their challenges.

Self-Consciousness: a heightened sense of awareness of oneself. It has commonly come to refer to a preoccupation with oneself, especially with how others might perceive one's appearance or one's actions. An unpleasant feeling of self-consciousness may occur when one realizes that one is being watched or observed, the feeling that "everyone is looking" at oneself. Some people are habitually more self-conscious than others. Unpleasant feelings of self-consciousness sometimes become associated with shyness or paranoia. When feeling self-conscious, one becomes aware of even the smallest of one's own actions. Such awareness can impair one's ability to perform complex actions. Adolescence is believed to be a time of heightened self-consciousness. A person with a chronic tendency toward self-consciousness may be shy or introverted.

Self-Pressure: self-pressure refers to the internal stress that individuals impose on themselves to meet their own expectations, standards, or goals. It's essentially self-imposed pressure, stemming from a desire to achieve, succeed, or avoid perceived shortcomings. While it can be a motivator for productivity and self-improvement, excessive self-pressure can lead to negative consequences like stress, anxiety, and burnout.

Sexism: the prejudice or discrimination based on one's sex or gender. Sexism can affect anyone, but primarily affects women and girls. It has been linked to gender roles and stereotypes, and may include the belief that one sex or gender is intrinsically superior to another. Extreme sexism may foster sexual harassment, rape, and other forms of sexual violence. Discrimination in this context is defined as discrimination toward people based on their gender identity or their gender or sex differences. Sexism refers to violation of equal opportunities (formal equality) based on gender or refers to violation of equality of outcomes based on gender (substantive equality). Sexism may arise from social or cultural customs and norms.

Sexual Assault: is an act of sexual abuse in which one intentionally sexually touches another person without that person's consent, or coerces or physically forces a person to engage in a sexual act against their will. It is a form of sexual violence that includes child sexual abuse, groping, rape (forced sexual penetration, no matter how slight), drug facilitated sexual assault, and the torture of the person in a sexual manner.

Toxic Masculinity: refers to harmful and exaggerated versions of traditionally masculine traits that can negatively impact men and society. It encompasses behaviours and attitudes that emphasize dominance, emotional suppression, and aggression, often leading to negative consequences for men's mental health and interpersonal relationships, while also contributing to issues like violence and social inequality.

Victim Blaming: occurs when the victim of a crime or any wrongful act is held entirely or partially at fault for the harm that befell them. There is historical and current prejudice against the victims of domestic violence and sex crimes, such as the greater tendency to blame victims of rape than victims of robbery if victims and perpetrators knew each other prior to the commission of the crime.